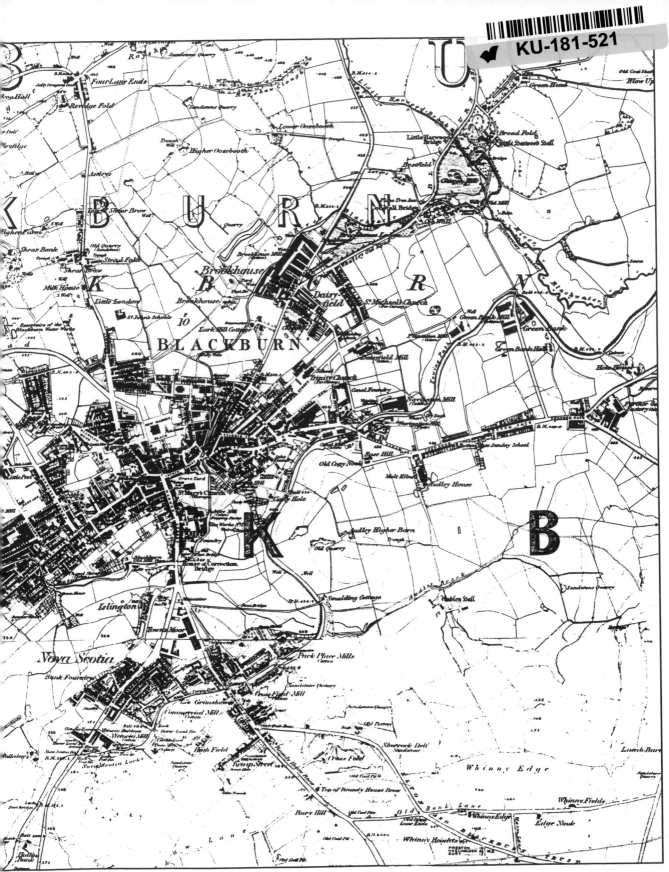

Blackburn in the 1840s.

BLACKBURN
A Pictorial History

Library
01254 292120

Gillies' map of Blackburn in 1822 (*see* illustration 8 and 16).

BLACKBURN
A Pictorial History

Geoffrey Timmins

Phillimore

1993

Published by
PHILLIMORE AND CO. LTD.,
Shopwyke Manor Barn, Chichester, West Sussex

ISBN 0 85033 865 4

Printed and bound in Great Britain by
BIDDLES LTD.
Guildford, Surrey

List of Illustrations

Frontispiece: 1822 map of Blackburn

Acknowledgements

I am particularly indebted to Ian Sutton and his staff at Blackburn Reference Library who provided most of the written and visual sources I required. Invaluable help was also given by Mike Millward, Curator of Blackburn Museum and Art Gallery; Mr. I. M. Willock, Plant Director, Philips Components Limited; Diana Winterbotham and her staff at Lancashire County Library Headquarters; and Mike Rothwell. Robin Whalley kindly undertook the onerous task of reading and correcting an early draft of the script, whilst Bill Cowell skilfully prepared the map reproductions. My wife, Carol, gave help and encouragement in numerous ways and has my especial thanks.

I gratefully acknowledge permission to reproduce the following illustrations:
Ian Baxter Professional Photography, 140; Blackburn Library, 8-14, 16, 18-21, 23, 25, 27, 29, 32, 33, 37, 38, 41-50, 53, 60-66, 68, 69, 71-78, 80-82, 84, 86, 88-114, 117-123, 125, 127-129, 131-134, 136, 137, 139, 143, 145-152, 154-171; Blackburn Museum and Art Gallery, 4, 6, 26, 34, 35, 51, 52, 58, 59, 83, 85, 87, 115, 116, 144, 153; Lancashire County Library Local Studies Department, 2, 3, 17, 28, 31; Philips Components Limited, 54-57; Mike Rothwell, 36, 141 and 142.

Introduction

Visitors to Blackburn have not always been complimentary about the town's appearance. Ralph Thoresby of Leeds, for instance, passing through on his way to the Preston Guild of 1702, could discover 'nothing remarkable' about either the town or its church.[1] Again, the diarist John O'Neil, who arrived in 1856, thought it 'the poorest looking place of a large town' that he had ever seen, there being 'no building of any importance except the Town Hall'.[2] Another mid-Victorian visitor, the journalist Edwin Waugh, was equally unenthusiastic. When he arrived on a 'wet and raw' morning during the depressed years of the Cotton Famine, he observed, with feeling, that the state of weather was 'one in which Blackburn does not wear an Arcadian aspect, when trade is good'.[3] And as recently as the 1960s, the eminent architectural historian, Nikolaus Pevsner, remarked that, for a town with a population of over 100,000, Blackburn might have done rather more to introduce civic dignity. 'As it is,' he maintained, 'the mills do all the impressing, especially when one looks down from the hills, and it is not architectural impressing'.[4]

At best, of course, summary views of this type provide extremely limited insights into Blackburn's past appearance or into the manner in which the town's built environment evolved. In fact, very little is known about either of these matters before the late 18th century. Not until then does a substantial amount of new information become available, a reflection of the importance Blackburn was attaining. Indeed, by the early Victorian era, the town had emerged as one of the largest and most populous in the country. This growth was associated particularly with the rise of the cotton textile industry, which reached its peak at the outbreak of the First World War. Plainly, the 19th and early 20th centuries are of particular significance in Blackburn's history and are worthy of detailed consideration.

In emphasising this period, however, it is important not to overlook both earlier and later phases in the town's evolution, nor to ignore changes that were taking place more generally. To do so would mean that the 19th- and early 20th-century developments cannot be viewed in context, so that their significance becomes hard to assess. Nor would it be possible to see how far the explanations for these developments were likely to have been unique to Blackburn, rather than applying to Lancashire towns in general.

With these considerations in mind, this book is divided into two sections. The first gives an outline of Blackburn's history, tracing its evolution from a remote settlement in Saxon times to a major town today, emphasising, in recent decades, the profound changes in its economic functions and in the appearance of its built environment. The second concentrates on the hundred-year period between the end of the Napoleonic era and the outbreak of the First World War. It examines the rapid expansion of the town, including the development of its early suburbs; the remarkable growth of its textile industry, with the numerous mills and terraced houses that it spawned; and the construction of its public and ecclesiastical buildings. As is so often the case in Lancashire, these developments, despite some ill-considered planning decisions, still provide the town with many of the more distinctive and stylish features of its built environment.

References

1. W. A. Abram, *A History of Blackburn* (1877), p.193
2. M. Brigg (ed.), *A Lancashire Weaver's Journal* (1982), p.22
3. E. Waugh, *Home Life of the Lancashire Factory Folk During the Cotton Famine* (1867), pp. 1-2
4. N. Pevsner, *The Buildings of England: Lancashire, the Rural North* (1969), pp.61-2

Blackburn's Development: An Overview

Little is known about Blackburn's origins and early history. Settlement existed on the site as long ago as Saxon times, but the earliest documentary evidence is obtained from the Domesday Survey of 1086.[1] This reveals that Blackburn had become a settlement of local importance, being one of comparatively few places in the Northwest to maintain a church. It was also a royal manor (the land having been held by Edward the Confessor) and gave its name to one of six wapentakes, or hundreds, into which the land between the Ribble and the Mersey was then divided for administrative purposes. Blackburn and three other royal manors apart, the land within the hundred was divided between 28 freemen, who paid rent and service dues to the king. The area was heavily forested, Blackburn manor itself containing a wood one mile long by one mile wide, the 'eyrie of hawks'.[2]

According to one authority, Blackburn's church, dedicated to St Mary, was already nearly 500 years old at the time of Domesday. It was altered in Norman times, though, boasting a magnificent porch which was

elaborately beautiful with zig-zag, and enric. d with mouldings and capitals, concentric arches, receding one behind another, and covered to the base with knot and drapcried sculpture, foliage and medallions, enclosing figures of the Virgin and the Holy Family.

Had this porch been viewed by Thoresby on his 1702 visit, he might well have formed a more favourable impression of the church. As it was, the church he saw was rebuilt in 1350 and renovated in 1540, a more fashionable Gothic st; le being preferred [1].[3]

The rebuilding of 1350 is one of the few developments known to have taken place in Blackburn during the late medieval period. It indicates, however, that the town was enjoying some prosperity, despite the toll that the Black Death must have taken at this time. Such progress was doubtless associated with Blackburn's function as a local market centre, but may also have arisen from an early interest in woollen cloth production. When this became commercially important locally is unknown, though there were fulling mills in north-east Lancashire at the end of the 13th century.[4]

The extent of such development should not be exaggerated, however. Throughout the late medieval era, Northwest towns remained small and the region was, as a whole, relatively backward and thinly populated. Besides, Blackburn lay remote from the main north-south route through the county. Accordingly, it lacked the trading advantages of Preston, Lancaster and Warrington, each of which was located on this route, as well as being near the head of a major river estuary. It is not altogether surprising, therefore, to find that Blackburn is not recorded on J. J. Bagley's map showing Lancashire towns which, before 1400, had been granted charters to hold fairs or markets.[5]

If Blackburn remained of no more than local importance during medieval times, it was certainly becoming a place of greater significance during the Tudor era. Evidence is still sparse, though both the renovation of the church in 1540 and the substantial sums raised during the

1580s to augment the endowment of the local grammar school, founded in 1514, point to the rising prosperity of local people.[6] Around this time, also, William Camden could report that Blackburn was a noted market town, whilst it is clear from contemporary accounts that an annual cattle and produce fair was being held on May Day.[7]

It is also reasonable to assume that, reflecting the situation more generally in Tudor Lancashire, the economy of the Blackburn area was becoming increasingly dependent on textile production. For much of this period, woollen goods predominated in the east of the county and linens in the west, with the Blackburn area occupying part of a transitional zone between the two.[8] Whether, as elsewhere, local families were moving into the manufacture of such new draperies as bays—a worsted and wool cloth—has not been confirmed.[9]

What is likely, however, is that the Blackburn area was at the forefront of the move into the production of fustians, a cloth comprising a linen warp and a cotton weft. This had certainly occurred by the early years of the 17th century, when nine fustian weavers from Blackburn and the neighbouring hamlets of Livesey, Witton and Mellor, were prosecuted when they failed to pay for raw materials supplied to them.[10] By the Restoration, the area was known for its production of fustian 'checks', the warp and/or weft of which was dyed before weaving, giving the finished product a checked or striped appearance. It may be that this cloth quickly gained a competitive edge, for, around this time, clothiers from the Blackburn area found that their customary freedom to trade at Preston market was denied and their cloth forcibly seized by 'agents of the monopolistic trading companies of that borough'.[11]

The rise of the fustian industry may have been strongly influenced by skills and fashions that Continental refugees brought to England during the latter half of the 16th century, though whether or not they actually settled in Lancashire is uncertain.[12] There were growing opportunities, too, in European markets as the long-established fustian industries of Italy and South Germany were displaced.[13] Also of importance were the advantages of Lancashire's damp climate in spinning and weaving vegetable fibres; the existing skills of the labour force in weaving linens; and the growing supply of labour available in the county to enable textile production to expand.

The additional labour needed by the expanding textile industry came partly from population growth. Walton's figures suggest that the number of households in the Blackburn Hundred increased from 2,657 in 1563 to 4,740 in 1664; an increase of 78.4 per cent. This was the second highest figure for all Lancashire hundreds, though considerably short of the 128.2 per cent increase for Salford Hundred.[14] It probably resulted largely from a rising birth rate, which, in turn, may have been a consequence of growing industrialisation. Evidence to support these contentions is hard to find, but the parish registers for Blackburn record an average of 145 baptisms between 1634-6, a third more than in 1601-13.[15] This figure is all the more impressive given the setback brought by the well-known population crisis of 1623. Thought to have been caused by harvest failure, its impact was widespread and, in Blackburn parish, recorded deaths reached 460, four-and-a-half times the average for the years 1619-21.[16]

Gaps in parish registration during ensuing decades make it hazardous to determine whether population increase was likely to have been maintained through the Civil War era. It is true that Blackburn's inhabitants escaped the worst ravages of the War. Even so, W. A. Abram has suggested that many of the twelve to fifteen hundred Parliamentary soldiers killed by Prince Rupert and the Earl of Derby after they captured Bolton in 1644 would have been recruited from the Blackburn area.[17]

The pressure that local population growth was exerting on Stuart Blackburn is indicated by the enclosure of the township's waste and common land. This took place in 1618 and

ı cloth finishing, especially those which required the application of water- or
hey included machines for printing cloth by means of engraved copper rollers.
veloped during the early 1780s at the works of Livesey, Hargreaves & Co.,
:, near Preston. This new technology began to supersede hand-block printing,
ın pioneered in Lancashire by Haworth, Yates and Peel, who opened their
rks at Oswaldtwistle, near Blackburn, in 1760.[27]
these textile factories were amongst the earliest in Lancashire, factory production
owly in Blackburn. As late as 1824, Edward Baines could report that it was only
: seven years that spinning had been carried on in the town and neighbourhood
iable extent. Even then, of 13 local cotton spinning firms he listed, two were
away at Hoghton and another was probably a supplier of yarn rather than a
ınes attributed this state of affairs to the loss of investor confidence following the
f Hargreaves' jennies in 1769 and of machinery at Wensley Fold spinning mill ten
But investment in factories was in any case hindered by the uncertain business
arose during the French wars.[29] Moreover, an insufficient supply of coal was
the locality to develop steam-powered mills on a substantial scale. This was so,
improvements brought to local transport as several of the main roads between
ınd neighbouring towns were turnpiked during the latter half of the 18th century.
matter was not resolved until the Leeds/Liverpool Canal was completed, joining
to Burnley and north-east Lancashire in 1810 and to Wigan and south Lancashire
, 5-9].[30]
ıwhile, the Blackburn area's major industry, textile weaving, continued to expand,
ıtrast to spinning and finishing, remained largely a domestic trade. This was partly
: technical shortcomings of the powerloom, but also to the ready availability of
labour. Between 1818-22, 55 per cent of the bridegrooms recorded in Blackburn's
ʒisters were described as weavers. Overall, the weaving labour comprised around
:ople, more than one quarter of the total population. Manchester and Bolton parishes
, it is unlikely that any other Lancashire parish achieved such high numbers as these.[31]
meet the needs of the hand weavers, considerable numbers of terraced cottages with
loor or cellar loomshops were built [10 & 11]. So, too, were numerous town-centre
ses, from which thread was distributed to hand weavers and to which the cloth they
d was returned [12]. For the most part, the warehouses belonged to firms of cotton
:turers who specialised in weaving. Most were probably small concerns, operating in
omary way by obtaining raw materials on credit from local or more distant merchants.
ır ranks also included such large-scale operators as Henry Sudell, John Hornby and John
all of whom were established merchants as well as manufacturers. Some manufacturers,
ɣ and Birley amongst them, eventually moved into spinning, as did William Feilden, a
:r of Blackburn's premier landowning family.[32]
ıs the cotton industry developed during the late 18th and early 19th centuries, Blackburn's
ıtion increased substantially. By 1821, it had reached 21,940, more than 80 per cent
the figure recorded at the first national census in 1801. House building virtually kept
with 1,780 additional dwellings being provided [13-15].[33] This led to a marked physical
ısion of the town, as is revealed by comparing Yates' 1786 map with those of Gillies
ł) and Hennet (1828-29). Much of this expansion resulted from the creation of hand
ers' colonies. In most cases, these comprised newly-formed streets grafted onto the edge
ʌn. This was so, for instance, in the cases of Cleaver Street and Moore Street on the eastern
ʒe and the Snig Brook and Nab Lane areas to the north. In other cases, most notably Nova

involved land at Revidge Moor, Whinney Edge an
'by reason of non-culture, yielded very little profit
the matter shared this view and recommended that t
rata amongst Blackburn's existing landowners.[18]
landowners were deprived of land to which they were
the enclosures added to the number of landless labou
labour force available for textile production.

Despite the growth of population in Tudor and St
settlement, having yet to attain even regional importan
in Lancashire, it does not appear amongst Hoskins' l
provincial towns in 1662.[19] Moreover, its physical size w
of Ralph Thoresby reveal. When he visited in 1702, he w
church whilst his dinner was being prepared.

By the time of Thoresby's visit, the Blackburn area
domestic textile production. Of the 109 bridegrooms record
between 1704-07, 48 per cent are given as weavers. That n
bridegrooms adds weight to the widely-held view that
occupation. As in earlier times, the weavers were living not
in the surrounding settlements, including Over and Little D
and Great Harwood.[20] Plainly, industrial activity in the loca
strong rural base.

To facilitate the emergence of rural production, a put
Merchants in Manchester and other towns took the risk of buyi
increasingly, Liverpool and of marketing the finished cloths. Th
on credit directly to families engaged in spinning and weaving
country middlemen. Known by various names, including fustian
manufacturer, these men put out the raw materials to domestic s
own localities, again giving credit.[21] Amongst this group was Wi
the man responsible for taking legal action against local fustian v

By the early 18th century, these manufacturers had begun to
fustian cloth in which the threads were not dyed prior to weavi
traditional 'checks'. The product, a plain printing fabric, was se
London, where the finishing trades were then centred.[22] Early ii
production are to be found in references dating from around 1720, w
in Blackburn with 'yarn crofts' adjoining. Here, yarn which had been
sour milk would have been exposed to the sun. In this way, bleachin

It was not until the later decades of the 18th century that the domina
was challenged. By then, technological advances in spinning machi
adoption of the water-frame and mule, produced cotton threads which v
be used as warps. Hence, the manufacture of an all-cotton cloth became c
At the same time, a local man, James Hargreaves of Stanhill, introduced
a hand-powered machine which produced weft thread. Despite early ho
which may have influenced Hargreaves' move to Nottingham, the machin
Lancashire, mainly, perhaps, in small workshops.[25]

The new spinning technology brought a strong impetus towards factor
Blackburn's earliest powered spinning mills being erected at Wensley Fold,
town, around 1778 [2] and at Spring Hill, Well Street, in 1797 [4].[26] So, t

developments i
steam-power. 1
These were de
Walton-le-Dal
which had be
Brookside W

Althoug
was adopted
within the la
to any appre
several mile
producer. B
destruction
years later.
climate tha
available i
despite the
Blackburn
In fact, the
Blackburr
in 1816 [
Mea
but, in cc
due to th
handlooi
parish re
15,000 r
excepte
Tc
ground
wareho
produc
manuf
the cu
But th
Birle
Horn
mem

popu
abov
pace
exp
(18
we
of
fri

Scotia and Grimshaw Park, on the southern outskirts, they comprised more distinct settlements, physically separated from the town [16-18].[34] Of course, compared with the settlement that mill construction was to generate, an issue dealt with in the following chapter, hand weavers' colonies had a very modest impact on Blackburn's development. Nonetheless, their contribution has generally escaped comment.

The town was also acquiring a veneer of elegance at this time, a reflection of the growing prosperity of its leading inhabitants. It could be seen in the construction of stylish, brick-built houses, especially in King Street, a number of which were occupied by textile manufacturers [19-22].[35] As Gillies' map reveals, several of these houses boasted sizeable gardens, formally laid out. New churches and chapels were also being erected, the most architecturally striking of which was St John's [23-27], whilst a major public amenity was provided when gas street-lights were introduced in 1819.[36] Meanwhile, to the west of the town, three of Blackburn's most prosperous townsmen, Henry Sudell and the Feilden brothers, William and Henry, built impressive mansions set in extensive parklands [28-32].[37]

Such developments met with the warm approval of certain contemporaries, including the journalist and historian, Edward Baines. Writing in 1824, he felt moved to observe:

> This place, at one time proverbial for its rudeness and want of civilisation, may now fairly rank in point of opulence and intelligence, with many of the principal towns in the kingdom.[38]

Whatever the truth of these assertions, Blackburn was certainly aspiring towards enhanced status, since, between 1801 and 1861, it rose from 29th to 21st position amongst England's most-populous provincial towns.[39] This growth continued to depend fundamentally on the development of the cotton industry, weaving especially. During the middle decades of the century, Blackburn's hand weavers were displaced, more quickly in the town than in the surrounding rural districts. In part, this change resulted from fundamental improvements made to the powerloom in the early 1840s by two Blackburn men, William Kenworthy and James Bullough. It was also a product of the massive investment in powerlooms that occurred during the major trade-cycle upturn of the mid-1840s.[40] This was closely associated with railway construction, which included the first line into Blackburn, from Preston, in 1846. By 1850, the town's rail links had been extended to north-east Lancashire, as well as to Bolton and Manchester [33-35].[41] This brought new opportunities to expand cotton production and, during subsequent decades, a major mill-building programme took place. As was generally the case in north-east Lancashire, weaving capacity especially was extended, with mills of a somewhat larger capacity being built [36-41].[42] By 1911, no fewer than 28,305 people in Blackburn were employed in cotton weaving, of whom almost two-thirds were female. They comprised more than a third of the total labour force, with the textile trades as a whole absorbing more than half [42].[43]

Amongst other manufacturing activity to develop in Blackburn during the 19th century, metal work and engineering, including textile machine making, was the most important. By 1911, this provided jobs for about 11 per cent of the town's male workforce. Other notable occupational groups were transport and construction, which respectively absorbed eight and seven per cent of male labour [43, 44], and domestic services, which gave employment to seven per cent of female workers. Plainly, Blackburn's dependence on a single industry was heavy, though less so for male than female employment, a situation that was only too familiar in Lancashire's weaving belt. Moreover, that some 90 per cent of the town's cloth production was sent to the Far East added strongly to the feeling expressed by some contemporaries that Blackburn's economy was not sufficiently diversified.[44] Even so, it should not be overlooked that a wide range of occupations was to be found in the town, with the professions, commerce, catering, woodworking and the dress trades all offering substantial job opportunities [45-48].

Blackburn's emergence as a major centre of cotton production brought an unprecedented increase in its physical size, as well as a profound alteration to the appearance of its built environment. Both these issues are dealt with in the following chapter, though it may be noted here that a fundamental change was brought to the layout of the town centre by the re-location of the market. This occurred in the mid-1840s, when the traditional site, at the junction of Church Street and Darwen Street, was abandoned and vacant land taken over on the east side of King William Street, a new thoroughfare opened in the mid-1820s as an extension of Preston New Road [49, 50]. It may also be noted that Blackburn's population showed a massive increase, the number of inhabitants reaching 133,052 in 1911, a sixfold increase compared with 1821. As was common in Victorian towns, a high birth rate, in part the consequence of a relatively young population, coupled with significant in-migration, was sufficient to counter appallingly high mortality rates.

Lancashire's cotton trade continued to expand until the First World War. However, the war years brought severe disruption to overseas sales. In Blackburn's case, the crucial Indian market in coarse cloths fell away dramatically, exports to that country rarely reaching half their pre-war levels of 3,000 million yards per annum and, by 1936, falling irrevocably to less than 500 million yards. This was partly the result of the rapid rise in India's own cotton industry, aided by tariff protection and the importation of redundant textile machinery from Britain. It was also the result of growing Japanese competition in the Indian market. Nor was the situation helped, it has been alleged, by the failure of textile entrepreneurs to innovate to a sufficient extent [51, 52].[45] Throughout these and subsequent decades overseas competition became more intense, surplus capacity remaining an ever-present problem, leading to a relentless programme of mill closure, aided, under the Cotton Industry Reorganisation Act of 1959, by government compensatory payments.[46] Between 1919 and 1936, no fewer than 79 of the town's 150 mills closed. By 1950, the number had shrunk to 50 and by 1983 to a mere five.[47]

Replacement industry, meanwhile, was developing, much of it the result of firms coming into the area rather than of local firms diversifying. They were attracted by the availability of relatively cheap labour, especially female, accustomed to factory work; by provision of new and existing industrial premises at low cost; and by the improved communications arising from the construction of a new ring road around the northern half of the town in the mid-1920s [53].[48] Amongst the most important of the new firms were Philips (later Mullards), who began to manufacture radio receiving valves in 1938 [54-57] and Scapa Porritt, who arrived in 1928 to make felts for the paper industry [58, 59].[49] The process of attracting new industry continued after the Second World War, helping to maintain a substantial manufacturing base in the town. By 1987, around a half of Blackburn's workforce was still employed in the manufacturing sector, a situation that was common throughout north-east Lancashire.[50]

Unfortunately, new industry did not generate sufficient jobs to replace those lost by the decline in textiles. This brought high levels of unemployment, which, along with an allegedly drab environment, low-quality housing and a 'weeping climate' prone to fog, frost and air pollution, encouraged out-migration.[51] This was especially acute during the 1930s, when the town's insured population fell by no less than 14.2 per cent.[52] By 1971, the total population had sunk to 101,825, only about three-quarters of the 1911 figure. In recent years, this decline has continued, despite the population having been bolstered by immigration, mainly from India and Pakistan.[53] This was stimulated by labour shortages in the 1960s and 1970s and, by 1981, immigrants amounted to about nine per cent of the total population.[54]

Only to a limited extent has replacement industry established itself in the town's redundant cotton mills, the general preference being for more accessible, modern buildings on the town outskirts. Indeed, few cotton mills now remain. Their demolition has inevitably brought a striking alteration to the Blackburn townscape, the impact on which has been made all the more dramatic by the comprehensive redevelopment of the town centre. This took place in the 1960s and '70s, providing a partly-enclosed shopping precinct; a new indoor retail market; a wholesale market; and a multi-storey town hall extension [60-62]. To create the space, the Victorian market hall and clock tower were demolished, along with most of the buildings to the south between Lord Street and Church Street and a vast tract of buildings to the north and east, enclosed by Victoria Street, Penny Street and Brown Street [63]. Major considerations behind the redevelopment were the additional revenue that would arise from utilising more fully the space occupied by the market place and the need to provide improved access for the rapidly increasing number of shoppers travelling in by car.[55] The degree of success achieved by the scheme is still debated [64-66], but its impact on the townscape is undoubted. Such an extensive range of starkly-functional, tile-clad buildings could scarcely contrast more strongly with the remainder of the town-centre buildings, both old and new. And this is the more so following the recent refurbishment of the town hall extension, giving it even greater prominence as a townscape feature [67].

But it is not only in the town centre that major redevelopment has occurred. During the last few decades, a massive housing programme has been implemented, designed to clear unfit dwellings and replace them with new ones. Several thousand houses were pulled down during the 1960s [68, 69], but, as late as 1973, no less than 14.8 per cent of the town's housing stock was still deemed to be unfit, the second highest figure for any Lancashire town.[56] Further large-scale demolitions took place during the 1970s and 1980s, despite the growing doubts expressed by those who, for a variety of reasons, preferred refurbishment of homes to demolition [70].[57] In recent years, though, both policies have been severely hit by public expenditure controls, leading to fears that the reduction in unfit dwellings may have been reversed.[58]

In order to accommodate the majority of the displaced families, new council housing estates were provided, occupying green-field sites on the town outskirts. Most were erected between the 1950s and 1970s, supplementing the limited amount of council housing that had already been provided during the inter-war years [71-76].[59] Meanwhile, the land made available from inner-area house demolition was used partly to provide sites for new dwellings, some in the form of high-rise blocks [77, 78], as well as for light industrial buildings, as in the Harwood Street area. Most of the latter, though, were to be erected on the town outskirts, where further industrial estates were provided, that at Shadsworth, with a designated area of 62.7 hectares, being by far the largest.[60] All were sited to take advantage of existing, or of planned, motorway links [79].

The changes that have occurred in Blackburn during the past few decades have had a fundamental impact on the appearance of the town. The desire to create an up-to-date, more attractive environment, both for townspeople and visitors, is only too evident in the extensive redevelopment that has taken place. Yet opinions will remain divided as to whether this was either necessary or desirable. It may be that much had to be done to ensure that Blackburn met changing needs and expectations effectively, but there are certainly many who regret the loss of some of the town's finest Victorian buildings, let alone its traditional, open-air market.

References

1. W. A. Abram, *A History of Blackburn* (1877), p.245; P.A. Whittle, *Blackburn As it Is* (1852), p.12.
2. Abram, *op.cit.*, p.47; J. J. Bagley, *A History of Lancashire* (1976), p.25.
3. Whittle, *op. cit.*, p.38; Abram, *op. cit.*, p.301.
4. A. P. Wadsworth and J. de L. Mann, *The Cotton Trade and Industrial Lancashire* (1931), p.4.
5. Bagley, *op. cit.*, p.44.
6. Abram, *op. cit.*, pp.322-24.
7. *Ibid.*, pp.248-49.
8. Wadsworth and Mann, *op.cit.*, p.24.
9. Ibid., pp.12-14.
10. Ibid., pp.36-37.
11. Abram, *op. cit.*, p.202.
12. A. P. Wadsworth, 'The Myth of the Flemish Weavers', *Transactions of the Rochdale Literary and Scientific Society* (1942), pp.59-60.
13. Wadsworth and Mann, *op. cit.*, pp.22-23.
14. J. Walton, *Lancashire, A Social History* (1987), p.25.
15. *The Registers of the Parish Church in Blackburn* (1911 transcription), pp.2-9.
16. *Ibid.*, pp.163-73.
17. Abram, *op. cit.*, p.145.
18. *Ibid.*, pp.256-60.
19. W. G. Hoskins, *Local History in England* (1959), p.177.
20. Lancashire County Record Office, Blackburn Parish Marriage Registers, 1704-07, PR 3073/1/4. The figures relate only to bridegrooms resident within Blackburn parish.
21. S. D. Chapman, *The Cotton Industry in the Industrial Revolution* (1972), pp.12-13; Abram, *op. cit.*, p.203; E. Baines, *History, Directory and Gazetteer of the County Palatine of Lancaster* (1968 reprint of 1824 edition) vol. 1, pp.504-05.
22. Abram, *op. cit.*, pp.202 and 230.
23. *Ibid.*, pp.293-94; Chapman, op. cit., pp.24-25.
24. A. E. Musson, *The Growth of British Industry* (1978), p.81.
25. Abram, *op. cit.*, pp.204-10; Wadsworth and Mann, *op. cit.*, pp.476-82; Musson, *op. cit.*, p.80.
26. Abram, *op. cit.*, pp. 230-31. The date for the Wensley Fold Mill is indicated by rights being granted in 1778 to convey water to the mill for a 49-year period (*Blackburn Mail*, 13 April 1795). By 1797, there was also a hand spinning mill in Union Street, which housed 14 jennies of 106 spindles each (*Blackburn Mail*, 3 May 1797).
27. For a detailed discussion of these developments, see Abram, *op. cit.*, pp.210-29.
28. Baines, *op. cit.*, pp.505 and 517-18.
29. M. M. Edwards, *The Growth of the British Cotton Trade, 1780-1815* (1967), pp.182-86.
30. Abram, *op. cit.*, pp.239-43.
31. G. Timmins, *The Last Shift* (1993), pp.33-38 and 44.
32. For details of these men, see Abram, *op. cit.*, pp.389, 399, 405 and 621-22.
33. Baines, *op. cit.*, p.502; *Blackburn Mail*, 24 April 1801.
34. Advertisements in the *Blackburn Mail* help to identify such colonies by recording the streets in which hand weavers' cottages could be found. The same paper notes that there were around 2,000 weavers at Nova Scotia, Grimshaw Park and Little Islington in 1826. Few would have been power weavers. See *Blackburn Mail*, 15 March 1826.
35. J. G. Shaw, *Bits of Old Blackburn* (1889), ch.3.
36. Whittle, *op. cit.*, pp.105-06.
37. Abram, *op. cit.*, pp.589, 662 and 759. See also R. D. S. Wilson, *The Feildens of Witton Park*, (n.d.), ch.2.
38. Baines, *op. cit.*, p.506.
39. Hoskins, *op. cit.*, p.178.
40. Timmins, *op. cit.*, pp.21 and 23.
41. Abram, *op. cit.*, p.244.
42. D. A. Farnie, *The English Cotton Industry and the World Market, 1815-1896* (1979), pp.286 and 301-08. The capacity of Blackburn's mills are given in M. Rothwell, *Industrial Heritage: A Guide to the Industrial Archaeology of Blackburn*, Pt.I (1985), pp.15-55.
43. 1911 *Census Report, Occupations and Industries*, vol. X, Pt.II (1913), pp.209 and 211.
44. D. Beattie, *Blackburn: the Development of a Lancashire Cotton Town* (1992), pp.26-27.

45. *Ibid.*, pp.144-46.
46. S. Pollard, *The Development of the British Economy, 1914-1967* (1960), p.422.
47. Beattie, *op. cit.*, p.167; Rothwell, *op. cit.*, p.5.
48. For comment on these matters with regard to the Philips concern, see *Blackburn Telegraph*, 27 August 1937 and 17 September 1937. The Blackburn Industrial Development Corporation played a leading role in persuading Philips to select the site for their new factory.
49. Scapa Dryers came to Blackburn because they were able to buy a disused skating rink, which gave them sufficient clear floor space to take their wide looms. See Scapa Dryers, Ltd., *Scapa News, Anniversary Number*, 1927-67, p.2.
50. *Lancashire at Work* (1991), p.32.
51. T. W. Freeman, H. B. Rodgers and R. H. Kinvig, *Lancashire, Cheshire and the Isle of Man* (1966), p.156; Beattie, *op. cit.*, pp.147-48.
52. G. S. Brown, *A Preliminary Plan of Lancashire* (1950), p.162.
53. Beattie, *op. cit.*, p.166.
54. *Ibid.*, pp.175-78; T. Moorhouse, 'The Newcomers', in *The Book of Blackburn* (1979), pp.99-110.
55. *Lancashire Evening Telegraph Markets Souvenir*, 31 October 1964, especially pp.8 and 18.
56. *Strategic Plan for the North West* (1974), p.110.
57. Beattie, *op. cit.*, pp.167-69.
58. Lancashire County Council, *The Lancashire Structure Plan; Explanatory Memorandum* (1987), p.22.
59. Beattie, *op. cit.*, pp.170-71; *Blackburn District Plan; Report of Survey* (1977), pp.14-15.
60. *Ibid.*, p.66.

1. This drawing of Blackburn parish church is by Charles Haworth, a local Victorian artist. It shows the church as it appeared after the 1540 restoration. A decorated style is apparent. The upper tracery of the east window has quatrefoil (four-leafed) openings, drawn into points at the top and bottom to give ogee arches. The tower and spire are rather squat and, unusually, the chancel is longer than the nave.

2. Wensley Fold Mill is shown on Yates' map of Lancashire, published in 1786. Yates marked water-powered mills with a waterwheel symbol, that at Wensley Fold being situated on the River Blakewater, immediately north of Witton Stocks.

3. The earliest map showing the route of the canal through Blackburn is that published by Charles Greenwood in 1818. A flight of locks was required at Nova Scotia, north of Hollin Bank, above which a level was maintained by taking a rather circuitous route along the southern slope of the Blakewater valley.

4. This engraving, dating from the 1880s, is Charles Haworth's impression of Spring Hill Mill around the time it was built. Sited on rising land to the east of Railway Road, it was a plain, functional building with two wings, each of three storeys. Steam-power was probably used from the outset.

5. Given the loss of water from using locks and from leakage and evaporation, water supplies in canals had to be constantly replenished. As this extract from the 1840s six-inch Ordnance Survey map demonstrates, reservoirs were built for this purpose, including that belonging to the Leeds and Liverpool Canal at Rishton, north-east of Blackburn.

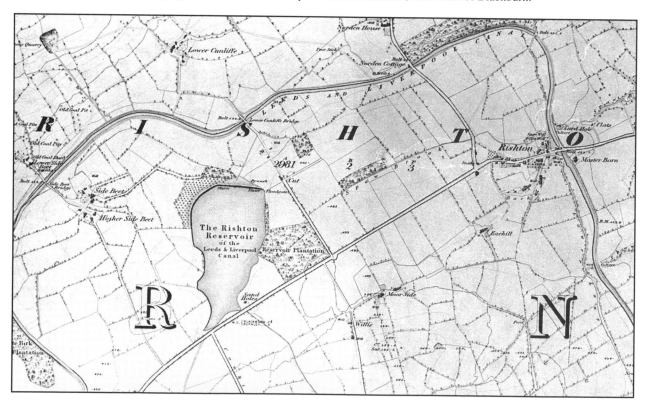

6. Below the locks, at Ewood, the canal level was maintained by constructing a high embankment. This passed over the River Darwen by means of a monumental aqueduct, the circular opening of which provided a particularly distinctive landscape feature. The illustration is again by Charles Haworth.

7. As this recent photograph reveals, the aqueduct is built in rock-faced stone, with concave flanking walls to support the embankment. Classical in style, it is a symmetrical structure with pilasters (built-in columns) at each corner and a cornice and parapet above. The road from Ewood to Witton was eventually built through the opening.

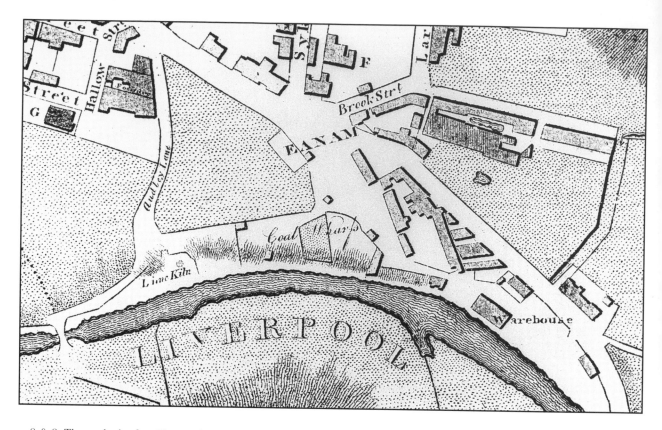

8 & 9. The coal wharfs at Eanam shown on Gillies' map of 1822 and on the 1840s five feet to the mile Ordnance Survey map, indicate the early importance of this commodity along the canal. However, cargoes recorded in *The Blackburn Mail* show that a wide range of goods was carried from the outset, including tallow, foodstuffs, timber and textiles.

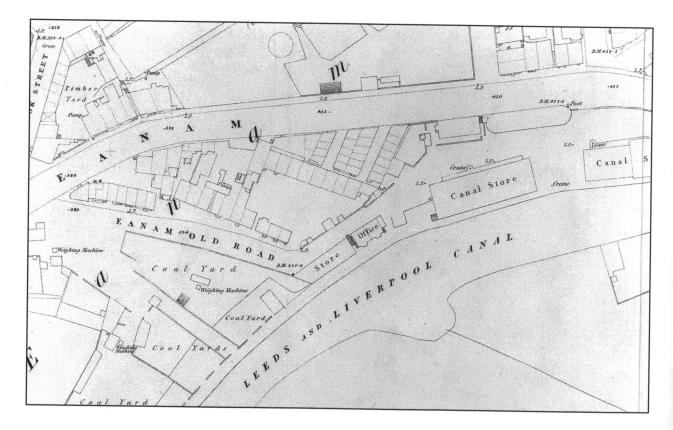

10 & 11. Natural lighting would be maximised when domestic loomshops were situated in upper storeys. However, since all but the coarsest vegetable fibres were best woven in humid conditions, cellar or ground-floor loomshops were generally preferred in the cotton and linen areas. Examples of former cellar loomshops, the windows of which were blocked after weaving ceased, are shown in the photographs, which probably date from the 1950s. They were in Cleaver Street and Larkhill Street.

12. This early warehouse was situated in Clayton Street and may well have been used by handloom manufacturers. Goods were hoisted to and from the taking-in doors on the first and second floors. Probably, the warps required by domestic weavers would have been prepared here.

13. Houses without loomshops in early 19th-century Blackburn were typically two-up, two-downs. The examples shown here were at Lunn Street, Wensley Fold. Strong vernacular qualities are evident, with local building materials·being used and decoration avoided.

14. Other examples of early 19th-century houses can be seen in this photograph of Water Street, between Penny Street and the Blakewater. Only the house second from the right has an original façade.

15. As in the case of the Lunn Street and Water Street examples, early two-up, two-downs normally had two chimney pots and hence two fireplaces. As this photograph reveals, these were located in the two front rooms, that downstairs being used as a general living room and kitchen. The photograph was taken in Haslingden Road during the mid-1980s.

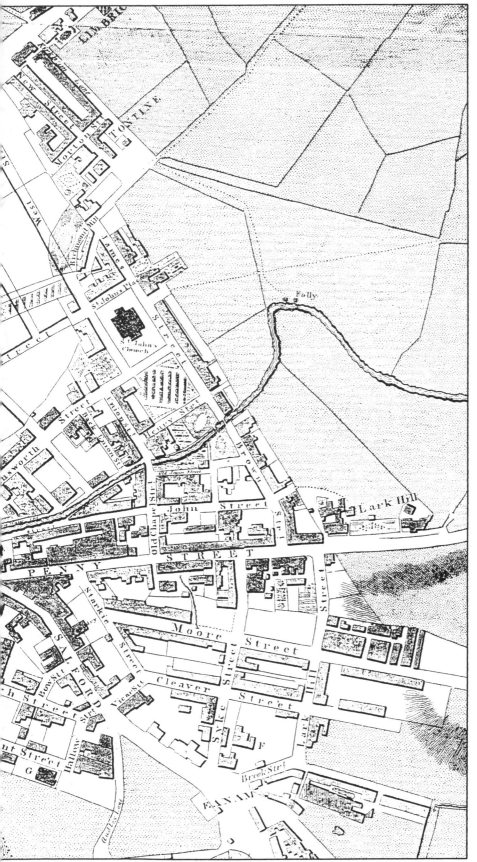

16. The 1820s maps, published by Gillies and Hennet, show a basically similar street plan to that of Yates, though quite a number of additional streets were constructed during the intervening period. On Gillies' map (*see also* frontispiece), which was drawn on the relatively large scale of 20 inches to the mile, the process of expansion is evident from the inclusion of several planned streets still awaiting development.

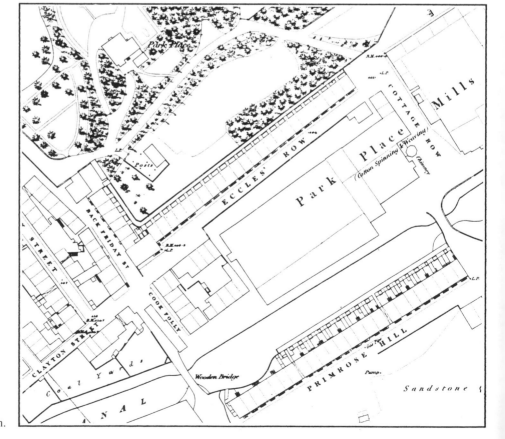

17. Hennet's map, published during the late 1820s, reveals further development, especially a completed Preston New Road, to the north west; Montague Street, on the west side of the town centre, linking new and old roads to Preston; and Whalley New Road, to the north.

18. Handloom weavers' colonies can often be identified on the 1840s five feet to the mile Ordnance Survey maps. The clearest examples show rows of small houses with steps to either the front and rear doors or to both. The Primrose Hill and Eccles Row examples were in the Grimshaw Park area of town.

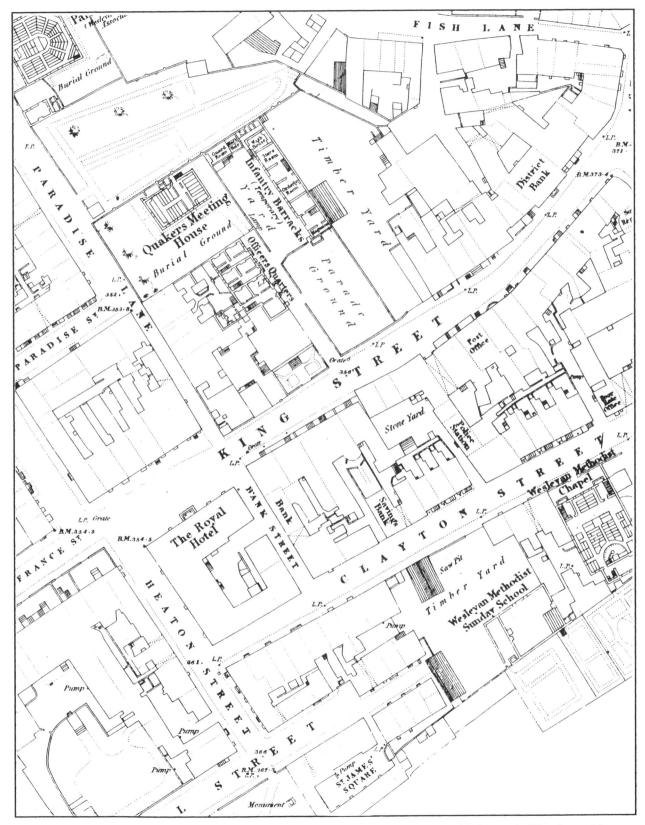

19. The 1840s five feet to the mile Ordnance Survey map reveals quite a number of sizeable houses in King Street. Most are shown with steps to the front door, indicating the provision of basements projecting above ground-floor level. Here, servants would have undertaken various domestic tasks, including cooking and clothes washing.

20. This photograph, dating from 1929, shows the block of houses at the junction with Bank Street. Brick-built, they were of a restrained classical style, two having lintels above the doorway, the other two having pediments. The nearest one at least had four storeys at the rear, the uppermost storey probably giving space for servants' bedrooms.

21. Probably taken in the inter-war years, this photograph shows the house built in 1778 by Bertie Markland, a merchant and calico manufacturer and later occupied by the Hornby family. It can be seen on the western edge of the 1840s map extract, with its distinctive flights of steps to the front door. The frontage has five bays, the central ones surmounted by a triangular gable with round-arched window opening. This feature complements the pediment above the door, which is supported on Ionic columns, the whole being set in a round-arched recess. The 1851 census returns reveal that the occupier of the house, William Henry Hornby, employed no fewer than nine resident servants, including a butler, a coachman, a groom and a cook.

22. This Haworth engraving shows another King Street house, this one opposite those shown in illustration 19. It was built by a local merchant, Richard Falkner, during the early 18th century. Classical in style, it had a five-bay frontage surmounted by an impressive balustrade. The garden was enclosed by a low wall fitted with decorative wrought-iron railings and was entered through a remarkably imposing pair of gateposts supporting ornate urns. Such a grand building certainly had a presence, though the expense of erecting it is thought to have ruined its owner. By the early Victorian period, barracks had been built at the rear of the house, as the 1840s Ordnance Survey map reveals. Further details are in J. G. Shaw, *Bits of Old Blackburn* (1889), chapter 3.

23 & 24. One of comparatively few classical-style churches to have survived in Lancashire, St John's, in Victoria Street, is of considerable architectural interest and importance. Most striking is its tower. The base is square and built from rusticated stone. Above is a smaller block with chamfered corners and ashlar faced. This gives way to an octagonal block, the decoration on which alternates between louvred, arched openings and pairs of columns. At the top is a plainer and still smaller octagonal block, with a balustrade at its base and domed roof surmounted by a weather vane. Appropriately enough, this features a weaver's shuttle. The church was opened in 1789 and the tower was added during the early 1790s. The drawing, with its rather curious perspective, is early 19th century.

25 & 26. Another late 18th-century church was St Paul's, in Nab Lane. Much more restrained in appearance than St John's, it was brick built with round-arched windows and a plain, square tower. The photograph was taken in 1950; the drawing is by Haworth.

27. Nonconformists, meanwhile, were also erecting places of worship, the earliest being the Baptist Chapel at Islington, opened in the mid-1760s. As the photograph shows, it was an unpretentious building, decoration being largely confined to round-arched windows with keystones. The chapel was demolished in 1930.

28. As can be seen from early 19th-century maps, the estates were sufficiently distant from the town to give seclusion, but not far enough away to cause undue inconvenience. The extract is from Hennet's map.

29. The size and style of the mansions is exemplified by Woodfold Hall, seat of Henry Sudell. Ashlar faced, it had a nine-bay frontage and a projecting portico with four plain columns.

30 & 31. Some idea of the splendid setting of these mansions can be obtained from Charles Haworth's drawing of Henry Feilden's Witton House and from early maps. As one mid-19th-century writer observed, Witton House stood on rising ground 'in the midst of rich plantations' and commanded 'some splendid views, affording every variety of scenery'. See J. G. Shaw, *Bits of Old Blackburn* (1889), chapter 17. Plantations were also extensive at Woodfold Park, where lakes provided an additional attraction.

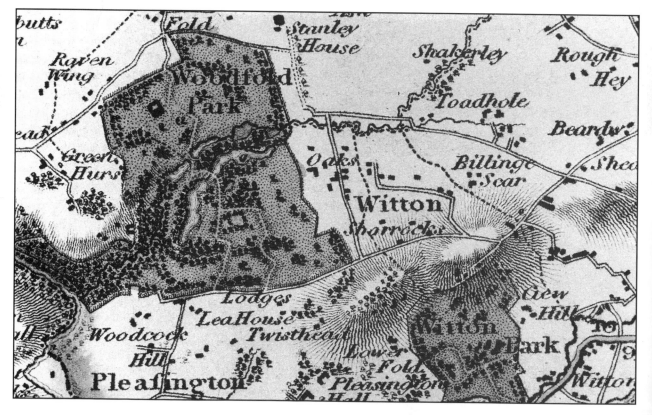

32. The social position of the families living in these mansions was high enough for them to attract visitors of considerable standing. Amongst those at Witton House were no lesser personages than the Prince and Princess of Wales, who breakfasted there on a visit to Blackburn in 1888. The photograph shows the royal couple leaving the house on their way to lay the foundation stone for the Technical School. For details, see R. D. S. Wilson, *The Feildens of Witton Park*, pp.34-35.

33 & 34. In the vicinity of Blackburn, the most spectacular engineering feat on the Preston to Blackburn line was the construction of the viaduct over the River Darwen at Hoghton Bottoms. Built from large blocks of rock-faced stone, it rises more than 100 feet above the river, spanning the valley in three, semi-circular arches. It took 18 months to build. According to one contemporary, it provided 'a dizzy view of the ravine below' (P. A. Whittle, *Blackburn As It Is* (1852), p.360). The photograph was taken about 1910 and the Haworth drawing is perhaps mid-Victorian.

35. Another Haworth drawing of the same period is of Cob Wall Viaduct, which took the railway to Clitheroe and West Yorkshire over the Blakewater Valley. The rural setting serves as a reminder that the physical expansion of Blackburn associated with textile mill settlement was by no means complete at this time.

36. Sheds used for power weaving were usually single storey, since, compared with multi-storey blocks, they gave a firmer foundation and greater uniformity in humidity and temperature. They could be lit from above by means of saw-toothed roofs, the glazed sections of which faced north to obtain the most uniform light. The roofs were angled steeply enough to prevent the sun's rays entering the shed directly, even in mid-summer. Details are in T. W. Fox, *The Mechanism of Weaving* (1922), pp.580-84. This shed was photographed in 1985 at Hollinshead Mill, St James Road.

37. Until the mid-Victorian years, though rarely later, cotton mill owners in Blackburn continued to build multi-storey spinning blocks, often in combination with weaving sheds. This aerial view of the Albion Mill in the early 1930s provides a good example. Moorgate Mill, a weaving establishment, is also shown.

38 & 39. These photographs give some idea of the external features of Blackburn's mid-Victorian spinning blocks. The first, at Rosehill Mill, Higher Barn Street, was built in the early 1860s, but no longer stands. Its four-storeyed, brick-built spinning block was a plain, functional structure, decoration being largely confined to a stone cornice supported by stone brackets. The second, of Waterfall Mills, Peel Street, shows the oldest block on the site. It dates from the early 1850s and is very similar in appearance to Rosehill Mill.

40 & 41. Multi-storey spinning blocks were often constructed with a framework of cast-iron columns supporting large wooden beams. These spanned the width of the building, supporting the floor joists and floor boards. A major problem, however, was that such mills were vulnerable to fire, which could result in complete destruction, as in the case of the examples shown. The engraving is of Swallow Street Mill, which burnt down in 1860 and the photograph is of Ordnance Mill in Coddington Street, which suffered the same fate in 1929.

42. The weavers shown here were employed at India Mill, Greenbank in 1930. The mill had been decorated to commemorate the wedding of the owner's son. As was generally the case, most of the women were young. At the 1911 census, almost half of Blackburn's female weavers were recorded as being under the age of 25 and some three-quarters under thirty-five.

43 & 44. Coal haulage would have occupied appreciable numbers in the transport category, not only because of the high dependency on coal as a domestic and industrial fuel, but also because local haulage services remained unmechanised. It was not until the inter-war years that the changeover occurred. Thus, when these photographs were taken in the late 1930s, the firm of Crook and Thompson still used some horse-drawn carts, but these had largely been superseded by motor wagons.

45. Amongst the woodworkers were those producing weavers' shuttles at the Addison Street works of Rowland Baguley & Co. The process made use of powered machinery in the form of belt-driven lathes, but hand techniques were still practised, some of them probably demanding appreciable levels of skill. The photograph was taken in the early 20th century.

46. This 1950s photograph taken at Bancroft's Intack works shows how the block of wood used to make the shuttle was hollowed out.

47 & 48. Some occupational groups remained the province of males, including the gas, water and electricity supply services, which employed 300 or so workers, and the production of 'spirituous drinks', which employed about two hundred. This would have been explained by the arduous nature of certain jobs in these industries, mechanisation generally being limited. Examples shown are in the retort room at Greenbank Gas Works in the early 20th century and the yard of Dutton's Salford Brewery, High Street, in the 1880s.

49. This Haworth drawing depicts Blackburn market in 1820, when it was still located at the junction of Church Street and Darwen Street. By early Victorian times, the site was becoming far too restricted to cope with the growing volume of trade and a new site was found on vacant land immediately north of the town centre.

50. The appearance of the new Market House is shown in this drawing dating from 1860. Classical in style, it had pairs of round-arched windows along the side and end walls and, at a higher level, window arcading. In front was an impressive clock tower, 72 feet in height. Its window arrangement repeated those on the main block and there were wide, open arches at the base. A fish market was situated on the south side.

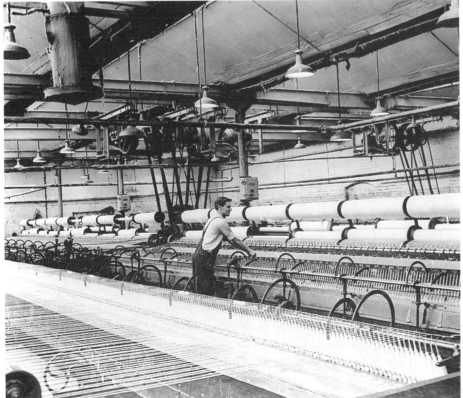

51. The continued use of traditional technology in Blackburn's cotton industry is exemplified by these mule frames at Didsbury Street Mill, photographed in the 1970s. Such machines had advantages over newer technology in terms of the range of yarns they could spin.

52. After the First World War, some, if relatively few, Blackburn cotton firms innovated, investing in automatic looms and ring frames. The Witton Mill Company, for example, installed these Sulzer shuttleless looms. This photograph dates from the 1970s.

53. Taken in the late 1920s, this photograph shows the double-carriage ring road at its junction with Whalley New Road. Plans had been made to use the central reservation as a tramway or light railway, though they did not materialise (D. Beattie, *Blackburn: the Development of a Lancashire Cotton Town* (1992), p.158).

54 & 55. The first photograph shows Philips' new factory being inspected after the foundation stone was laid in March 1938. The second is of the completed building, its steel frame encased by low brick walls and narrow window piers. This gives a high ratio of window to wall space, thereby ensuring good natural lighting.

56 & 57. These early photographs taken at the Philips' works show the workforce, indicating the importance of female labour to the firm, and the main product, a reminder of the transformation that was taking place in home entertainment during the 1940s and 1950s.

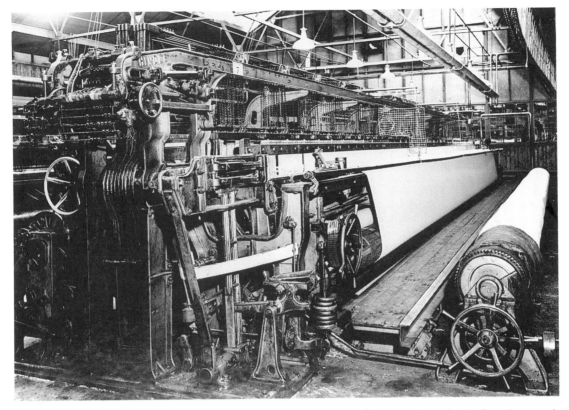

58 & 59. To make paper dryer felts, extremely wide looms were used of the type shown in the first photograph. It was taken at Scapa Works, probably in the 1950s. The wide looms required equally wide healds, used to raise the warps in the loom. An example is shown in the second photograph, being delivered to the Scapa Works, probably in the 1930s.

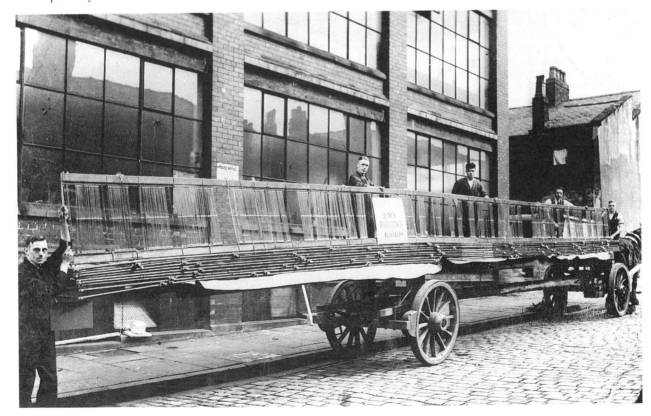

60-62. This sequence of 1960s photographs, the first two looking south towards the cathedral, shows the construction of the shopping precinct and town hall extension. Property beyond the development area, in Lord Street, including Thwaites' Arcade, awaited demolition, as did the shops to the left in Victoria Street.

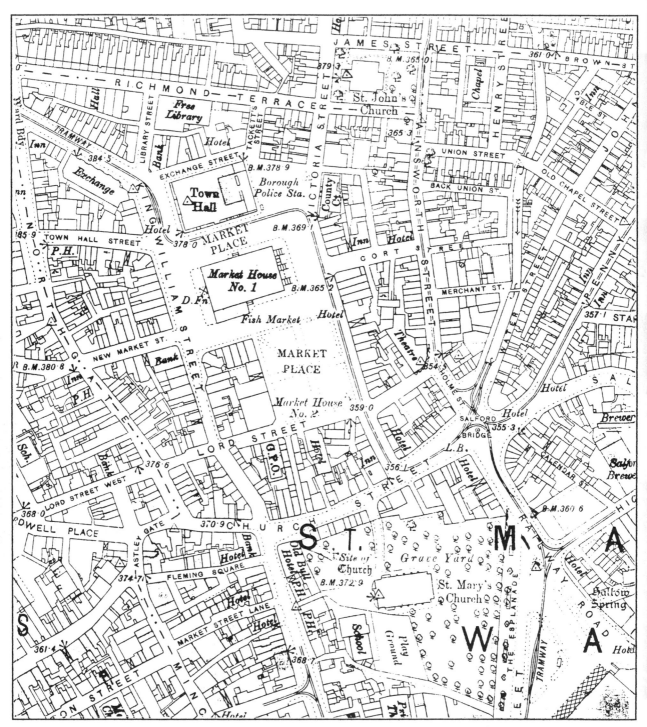

63. The extent of the demolition area can be gauged from this extract from the 1890s 25-inch Ordnance Survey map.

64. The changes arising from the redevelopment for both shoppers and stallholders are illustrated by comparing the 1950s photographs of the old market hall and the stalls outside, with the interior of the new retail market in illustration 65.

65 & 66. In the photograph above, the interior of the market is certainly lighter and more spacious than the interior shown in illustration 64 and, compared with outside trading, more comfortable. Traditionalists, though, will argue that the loss of the indefinable quality of old markets, often referred to as 'atmosphere', has been too high a price to pay.

67. The extension maintains a functional appearance but, beyond that, there has been little attempt to make it blend with the 1960s architecture, let alone that from earlier periods.

68. Amongst the early demolition was that in the Montague Street clearance area. This photograph of Feilden Street serves as a stark reminder of the disruption it brought to local community life and facilities.

69. This photograph is of William Henry Street, also in the Montague Street clearance area. Together with the Feilden Street photograph, it indicates the scale on which demolition took place.

70. Refurbishment of 19th-century terraces has been accompanied by environmental improvements, including provision of open spaces, tree planting, and the creation of one-way streets. The example shown is in the Audley Range area.

71 & 72. These examples of early council housing, taken around 1930, are at Brownhill and Roe Lee Park. Instead of long, fairly uniform terraces laid out in a grid-iron pattern of streets, the preference was for semi-detached houses and short terraces, which were set at angles to one another and which showed marked variation in appearance.

73. Photographs of early council housing often demonstrate the influence of the Garden City movement, in this case showing the attractive setting of the Roe Lee houses around the circular park area (laid out in 1925).

74. In addition to the park, facilities which developed at Roe Lee included a primary school, the classrooms of which opened onto a covered verandah.

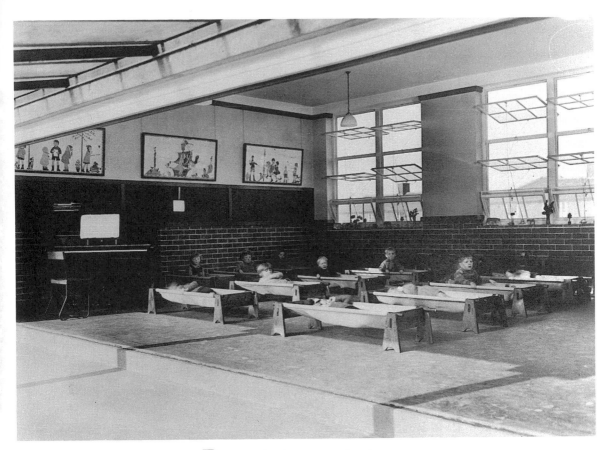

75. The school evidently offered a comprehensive range of facilities for its pupils.

76. St Gabriel's Church was another facility provided at Brownhill. It is brick built, with a square, rather plain west tower and pairs of extremely narrow, round-headed windows along the nave.

77. The photograph shows high-rise flats at Larkhill when they were near completion in 1964. The contrast they offered in living style compared with the traditional terraces surrounding them was stark and inevitably they provoked strong reactions.

78. Part of the Larkhill redevelopment was the visually-striking health centre. A functional, modern-movement building of brick and reinforced concrete, the upper storey overhangs the lower, part of which is open. Thin concrete window divides, which project slightly, offer an effective vertical counterpoint in a building with such a strong horizontal emphasis.

79. This photograph of the Whitebirk Industrial Estate was taken in 1993. It shows steel-framed buildings, usually clad with ridged steel sheets. For the most part, architectural relief on such developments is confined to variations in colour and in the direction of the sheet ridging.

Victorian and Edwardian Development

Comparison of Gillies' 1822 map of Blackburn (*see* frontispiece) with that of the six-inch to the mile Ordnance Survey map of the 1840s (front endpaper) reveals clearly the impact of early factory industry on Blackburn's development. Particularly notable are the emerging mill colonies at Brookhouse (north-east of the town centre); at Grimshaw Park and Nova Scotia (on the southern fringes); and in the Whalley Banks area (to the south-west) [80, 81].[1] The Brookhouse and Whalley Banks mills were located in the Blakewater valley, whilst those at Nova Scotia and Grimshaw Park were adjacent to the canal. Both types of location gave relatively cheap building land beyond the town centre, as well as water for steam raising. Additionally, canal-side locations offered the prospect of direct loading and unloading of goods, whilst river-valley sites provided high humidity levels, a consideration of no little importance in cotton production.[2] Nor should it be forgotten that these sites were all established industrial centres, mostly of handloom weaving, before they acquired cotton spinning and weaving mills.[3] Some useable premises and labour would thus have been available to entrepreneurs as the older activities declined.

Further map comparisons, this time of the 1840s and 1911 six-inch Ordnance Survey maps (front and rear endpapers), demonstrate the remarkable degree to which factory settlements, some of which diversified their manufacturing activity beyond cotton production, continued to develop in Blackburn during Victorian and Edwardian times. The early industrial colonies on the town outskirts expanded further, whilst many new mills and their associated settlements were created, mainly spread out along the canal and, from the 1840s, the railway [82, 83]. In consequence, not only did the physical size of the town increase, but, as in the Salford area, the available space within it became fully utilised [84-89]. To a large extent, Blackburn became a town of mill settlements, laid out in grid-iron streets, and welded together into a dense urban mass.

The inhabitants of these emerging settlements developed their own community identity centering on such basic social amenities as schools, places of worship, shops, sports clubs and public houses. They did so, too, with regard to workplace, a feeling which their employers sought to enhance by encouraging deferential attitudes and by providing such paternalistic treats as seaside outings.[4] At the same time, Blackburn's working-class people had the opportunity, if not always the means or inclination, to take advantage of a growing range of amenities which served the town as a whole. Amongst them were trams and railways, which greatly improved the ease and distance they could travel, as well as the cost of so doing [90-92]; the town-centre market [93-96] and shops [97-100], which extended the range of their shopping options; and leisure facilities, which, at the one extreme, enabled them to take healthy perambulations in Corporation Park [101-106] or Queen's Park [107-110] and, at the other, to enjoy the immensely popular, if, in some contemporary eyes, the rather unseemly entertainment provided by the music halls [111, 112].[5] Moreover, a broader civic identity was fostered in the local communities by such developments as the granting of parliamentary representation to the town in 1832 and of borough status in 1851.[6] And there can be little doubt that civic identity was also promoted by major events in which the whole town could take pleasure, not least the historic F.A. Cup Final victories of Blackburn Olympic in 1883 and of Blackburn Rovers on no fewer than five occasions during the mid-1880s and the early 1890s [113, 114].[7]

Such landmarks in Blackburn's development were understandably a source of considerable pride amongst contemporaries. Even so, there were those who did not always take an uncritical view about the way in which their town was developing. This is most evident with regard to public health matters and is well exemplified by the squalid living conditions so graphically reported by John Withers in 1853. Particularly telling are the statistics he provides on house sanitation. No doubt taking the worst cases, he reports that the inhabitants of 1,165 houses (about 15 per cent of the entire housing stock) shared a mere 246 privies, an average of nearly five houses, or some 25 people, per privy. Streets in a worse than average position included Freckleton Street, with 35 houses and five privies; Queen Street, which had 17 houses but only one privy; and, most disturbingly, Cockcroft, where there were 37 houses and no privies.[8]

Ideally, Withers wanted each house to have its own water closet. Before this could be achieved, though, radical improvements were required to the town's drainage system. According to Withers, comparatively few house drains had been installed and those that existed fed into sewers constructed on the 'worst possible principle, being generally square, or of a rectangular form, and built of dry Rubble'. Seepage was inevitable. Even more disgusting was the condition of the river Blakewater, into which the sewers drained. In itself, this was a major health hazard, but it was made worse by several weirs built across the river for industrial purposes. These reduced the natural scouring properties of the river and blocked the sewage when the river was low. The only adequate solution, Withers maintained, was the construction of a new sewer at a lower level than the river bed. This would terminate at Pleasington, to the west of the town. Here, rather alarmingly, the sewerage could be distributed through pipes over the surrounding land, the 'natural productivity' of which would thereby be enhanced.[9] It was a utilitarian scheme of which Edwin Chadwick, that most eminent of Victorian public health reformers, would have wholeheartedly approved, at least in principle.[10]

In the event, a rather different scheme emerged during the 1860s. It comprised the construction of a new intercepting sewer from Salford bridge to Witton, along with an outlet works with three settlement tanks at Witton and a sewage farm further west at Hoghton. By 1877, expenditure on these improvements exceeded the sizeable sum of £200,000.[11] However, continuing population growth soon rendered even this provision inadequate and, in 1875, land was purchased at Samlesbury, near Preston, to develop a much bigger sewerage works. By 1901, two 24-inch pipes were depositing an impressive five million gallons of sewage per day into 16 settlement tanks. Students from Blackburn College who visited the works at this time were shown a glass of the clear water that emerged at the end of the treatment process. Not surprisingly, they declined the opportunity to sample it.[12]

Improvements in Blackburn's sewerage system depended, of course, on adequate supplies of water being available. This may not have been the case until the mid-1840s, when Blackburn Water Company, reconstituted in 1844, built new reservoirs at Pickup Bank, Guide and Hoddlesden. These provided a combined storage capacity of 180 million gallons, but soon proved insufficient. Accordingly, Daisy Green reservoir was constructed in 1849 and Audley reservoir in 1856, each holding around 12 million gallons. Even this capacity, however, could not satisfy the demands of Blackburn's rapidly-growing population, which, during the third quarter of the century, more than doubled its water consumption to two million gallons a day. A partial solution was found by erecting Fishmoor reservoir in 1868, which could store 310 million gallons of water, thereby increasing the capacity of Blackburn's local reservoirs some two-and-a-half fold. However, the problem of ensuring that these reservoirs were kept as full as possible still remained and it was for this reason that parliamentary approval was obtained in 1877 to take water from the rivers Brennand and Whitendale in the Forest of Bowland, some 20 miles to the north. The first supplies from this source were fed into Fishmoor reservoir in 1882, a 30-inch diameter main being provided which was capable of delivering eight million gallons a day [115-117].[13]

With improved sewerage and water supply systems in place, equipping Blackburn's houses with water closets became a real possibility. Yet, probably because of the cost involved, this proved to be a protracted affair. No doubt the problem of shared privy accommodation was gradually overcome, but as late as 1891, there were still as many as 11,500 houses (43 per cent of the total) which depended on excreta tubs for sanitation and a further 4,346 (16 per cent) on the even more insanitary privy-middens [118, 119]. Only 5,921 houses (22 per cent) were fitted with water closets.[14] Admittedly, this figure grew substantially in the years leading up to the First World War, but, as late as 1891, some 11,500 excreta tubs remained in use.[15] Another decade was to elapse before they were virtually eliminated.[16]

There can be little doubt that insanitary housing, which was always likely to encourage disease, contributed appreciably to the high levels of mortality in Victorian Blackburn. Between 1885-90, the town's death rate averaged 24 per thousand, still above the rate which, a generation earlier, had been deemed as the level high enough to necessitate the establishment of a local board of health. Further, amongst 28 of the country's largest towns, only four were less favourably placed. Even more disturbing was the town's infant mortality rate, which stood at a staggering 244 per thousand or about one in four. Amongst the leading 28 towns in 1891, this figure was only exceeded in Preston and Leicester.[17] Apart from inadequate sanitation, Blackburn's medical officers of health, in common with their counterparts elsewhere, attributed such high infant mortality to a variety of causes, laying stress on the inadequate feeding of infants and on mothers returning to work too soon after giving birth.[18]

Considerations of this type point to high levels of social deprivation, which become all the more evident when mortality figures for different parts of Blackburn are compared. Thus, in St Mary's Ward, located in the central area of town, the infant death rate exceeded 215.4 per thousand between 1902-11. In marked contrast, the corresponding figure for St Silas' Ward, to the west of the town centre, was only 92 per thousand.[19] By this time, mortality levels in the town as a whole had diminished to a notable degree,[20] but the persistence of such marked local variations demonstrates that, in health matters, much remained amiss in Blackburn's densely-populated mill communities.

The relatively low mortality figure for St Silas' Ward serves as a reminder that not all the housing erected in Victorian Blackburn was crowded and insanitary. Indeed, it was within this ward that Blackburn's middle-classes chose increasingly to live. Here they constructed numerous detached or semi-detached houses, especially along Preston New Road and the streets bordering Corporation Park [120-123]. In part, this development arose from a need to obtain more building space for the growing number of middle-class families. During the early Victorian era, this could still be found close to the town centre, as in the case of Richmond Terrace, erected in the late 1830s [124]. Increasingly, however, the demands of an expanding central business district proved overwhelming and middle-class housing was converted to provide offices for solicitors, accountants, architects and so on. By the late 1870s, J. G. Shaw could report that most of Blackburn's leading families had moved out of the town centre to the western suburbs.[21]

Not all of them moved far, however. Many of their houses were situated well within comfortable walking distance of the town centre, even allowing for the hilly terrain. For those moving further out, personal carriages might be available, supplemented, from the 1880s, by tramways. Indeed, access to and from town was made all the easier by the even and relatively gentle gradient of Preston New Road [125, 126]. It may also be noted that the area was elevated above the town centre, with the prevailing winds blowing the domestic and industrial smoke away to the east. Accordingly, Blackburn's middle-class families could live in an area which was not only healthy and provided a reasonable degree of exclusiveness, but which, in large measure, remained convenient for town-centre facilities.

It is important to remember that housing improvements in Victorian and Edwardian Blackburn were by no means confined to those at the highest levels in society. Under the stimulus of bye-law provisions and a general rise in real incomes, much better-quality terraced housing was also being erected, most of it on the town outskirts. By the late 19th century, the best of it could offer a range of desirable facilities, including cavity walls, a fireplace in each room, an outside water closet and a front parlour [127, 128]. As yet, however, only a minority of families could afford such dwellings; for all too many, the new standards being set had to await the provision of subsidised housing after the First World War.

Improved housing could add appreciable architectural value to Blackburn's built environment. But it should not be overlooked that many buildings within the town's mill communities were by no means lacking in style and pretension. Indeed, they might even be regarded as visually impressive. This is most evident in the case of churches and chapels, quite a number of which were erected from the end of the Napoleonic Wars onwards [129-132].[22] Finance mainly came from public subscription, though funds to build St Peter's church, consecrated in 1821, were obtained from the post-war parliamentary grants for church building,[23] whilst the parish church of St Mary, rebuilt during the 1820s, was partly financed by a church rate levied on Blackburn's inhabitants [133-138]. Not surprisingly, this was a measure that did not meet with universal approval.[24] The yards of the new churches gave much-needed burial space, though the provision of large, open pits for burying paupers says much about the lack of compassion amongst those who allowed it [139].[25]

On occasions, architectural interest in Blackburn's mill communities could extend to the mills themselves, two of the finest examples being Cicely Bridge Mill, erected 1860-63 [140] and Imperial Mill at Greenbank, dating from 1900-1 [141-143]. The former, demolished a few years ago, was a stone building with pronounced quoins and an elegant cornice held on paired brackets. The latter, which still stands, is a massive structure of red brick, architectural variation being provided by lighter-coloured courses above the windows. Its twin water towers, housing tanks for the sprinkler system, are capped by ornate copper domes.

As would be expected, however, the Victorians and Edwardians erected the greatest concentration of their finest buildings in and around the town centre, with the customary contest between revived Gothic and classical styles being evident. With regard to buildings in the former style, the major survivors are the library and museum (1874) [144-148] and, more obviously, the Cotton Exchange (1865) [149-152]. Those in the latter style are more numerous, the most notable examples being the Town Hall (1856) [153-157]; the railway station (1888) [158 & 159]; the Old Bank (1878) [160]; the Technical School (1888-91) [161]; and the post office (1907-8) [162]. To this group may be added the demolished Market House with its prominent tower; the police station and sessions court, opened in 1912 [163]; and the adjoining public halls, completed in the early 1920s [164-166]. Such buildings bring no little architectural distinction to the town centre, though this would have been far more apparent had they been grouped closer together and had they not had to compete with the sheer dominance of the 1960s redevelopment [167-171].

Plainly, then, Blackburn's development during Victorian and Edwardian times brought notable improvement to the appearance of the built environment, especially with regard to ecclesiastical and public buildings. At the same time, public utilities were gradually improved; housing standards enhanced; and the range of civic amenities extended. Even so, the rapidity with which the town grew imposed severe and unrelenting pressures on the quality of its built environment, especially with regard to housing and to public health facilities. Moreover, periodic downturns in trade, with the high levels of unemployment they brought, could plunge vast number of families into abject poverty, from which recovery might be a long drawn out affair. On balance, the quality of life for most families in Blackburn's mill communities probably improved during Victorian and Edwardian times, but all too many of them continued to live in cramped and insanitary houses, breathing air contaminated by smoke from domestic and industrial fires and suffering illnesses which could still cause a disturbing number of fatalities, especially amongst infants.

References
1. J. D. Marshall, 'Colonisation as a Factor in the Planting of Towns in North-West England' in H. J. Dyos, *The Study of Urban History* (1966), pp.226-28.
2. D. A. Farnie, *The English Cotton Industry and the World Market* (1979), pp.48-51.
3. See illustration 18, for example.
4. These matters are discussed in P. Joyce, *Work, Society and Politics* (1980), chs.2 and 3.
5. See D. Beattie, *Blackburn: the Development of a Lancashire Cotton Town* (1992), p.115.
6. W. A. Abram, *A History of Blackburn Town and Parish* (1877), pp.372-77.
7. Their successes in the F.A. Cup competition are noted in A. Holliday, *Blackburn in Retrospect* (1975). This book contains an interesting collection of historical illustrations of Blackburn, as does P. Worden and R. Whalley, *Blackburn in Old Picture Postcards* (seventh edition, 1992).
8. J. Withers, *Report on the Sanitary Condition of the Borough of Blackburn* (1853), p.29.
9. *Ibid.*, p.70.
10. See, for example, E. C. Midwinter, *Social Administration in Lancashire, 1830-1860* (1969), pp.67-68.
11. Abram, *op. cit.*, p.380.
12. Blackburn Reference Library, *Notes on Sewage Disposal and the Samlesbury Sewage Works, 1869-1926.*
13. *Barrett's General and Commercial Directory of Blackburn and District* (1951), pp.6-7.
14. *Notes on Sewage Disposal ... 1869-1926.*
15. *Ibid.*
16. Beattie, *op. cit.*, p.157.
17. *Annual Report Upon the Health of Blackburn for the Year 1891* (1892), pp.8 and 10.
18. For example, the 1902 Report (p.28) maintains that infants were given foul feeding bottles and improper food at irregular intervals.
19. *Annual Report Upon the Health of Blackburn for the Year 1911* (1912), p.44.
20. *Ibid.*, p.28.
21. J. G. Shaw, *Bits of Old Blackburn* (1889), ch.3.
22. Details are given in Abram, *op. cit.*, pp.351-70.
23. Church financing is considered in Beattie, *op. cit.*, pp.133-34.
24. See G. C. Miller, *Blackburn, the Evolution of a Cotton Town* (1951), pp.150-57.
25. Withers, *op. cit.*, pp.26-27.

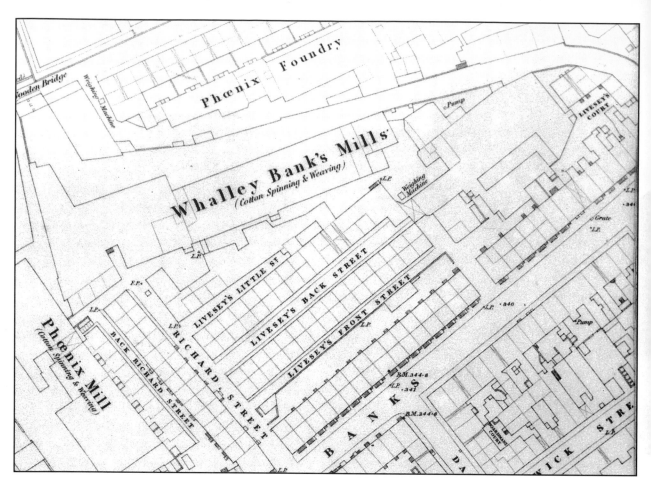

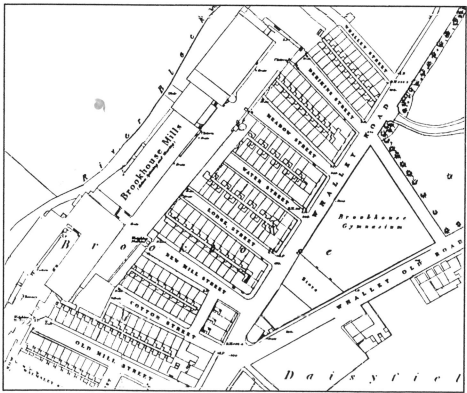

80 & 81. The quality of housing in the early mill colonies varied appreciably, as these extracts from the 1840s five feet to the mile Ordnance Survey map make clear. In the Whalley Banks settlement, several blocks of back-to-backs are evident to the north of the main road, whilst the through houses opposite were grouped around confined yards or courts, access to which was by means of narrow tunnels placed at intervals between the houses. By contrast, the Brookhouse settlement consisted almost entirely of through houses, with back passages provided to facilitate waste disposal. Even here, though, back yard provision was less than generous and houses were built at one end of successive rows, so that the back passage they shared may not have been open at either end.

82 & 83. The mill colonies produced a striking townscape dominated by starkly functional, multi-storey spinning blocks and tall, round-sectioned mill chimneys. The inter-war photograph taken from Nova Scotia locks and the Haworth drawing of the area to the east of Eanam Wharf in mid-Victorian times give some impression of this townscape, though Haworth has surely over-emphasised the size of the Old Windmill, built in 1822.

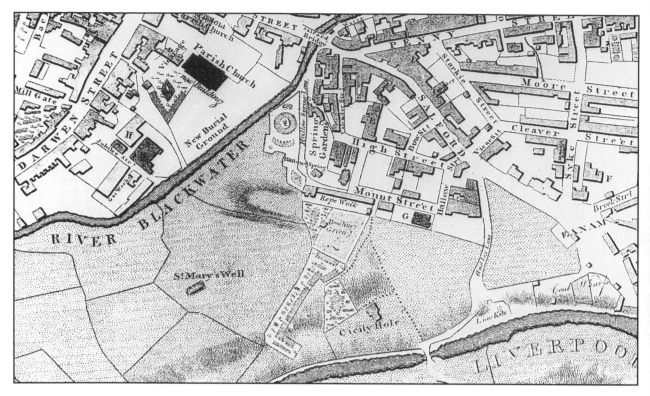

84. One major development within the town stemmed from the need to provide adequate access to the railway station. This was to be located immediately south of Mount Street, so that, as the extract from Gillies' 1822 map reveals, the most obvious route to choose was that along Hollow Spring Lane, to join with the main road system at Salford Bridge.

85. This Haworth drawing shows the view from Salford Bridge looking south-east towards the site of the proposed railway station before it was built. Spring Hill Mill can be seen in the background. In improving the Hollow Spring Lane route, the problem arose of channelling additional traffic generated by the railway across a narrow bridge, already heavily used.

86. The solution adopted was to demolish the old bridge and replace it with a new, flat one, which extended 250 feet along Hollow Spring Lane. Subsequent extensions of this bridge helped to create the triangular area of flat land in front of the station bordered by Railway Road and the Boulevard. This became the focal point for Blackburn's public transport system, as is evident from this 1920s photograph. Electric trams, charabancs, taxis and motor coaches are all on hand to meet passenger needs.

87. Extensive rebuilding accompanied the replacement of Salford Bridge, resulting in the scene depicted in this drawing. Again by Haworth, it is taken from a vantage point a little to the east of that showing the old bridge and reveals a dramatic transformation in the townscape. The changes met with the strong approval of J. G. Shaw, editor of the *Blackburn Times*, who was particularly impressed by the ranges of 'lofty and well-proportioned buildings'.

88. This photograph, taken around 1906, views Salford from the opposite direction. The impressive circular façade of the classical-style *Bay Horse Hotel*, occupying the corner of Water Street and Salford, is prominent.

89. Much of the redevelopment in the Salford area was sanctioned by an Improvement Act, obtained by Blackburn Corporation in 1882. The photograph, taken to present as evidence of the need for redevelopment, shows Salford looking towards the bridge. As the main easterly route in and out of the town, it was extremely narrow (certainly lacking the width to take a tramway) and was closely bordered on either side by houses and other buildings.

90. Blackburn's tramway system was established during the 1880s. At first, the Corporation's preference was for horse-drawn vehicles, the example shown here being photographed at Billinge End on the Preston New Road route.

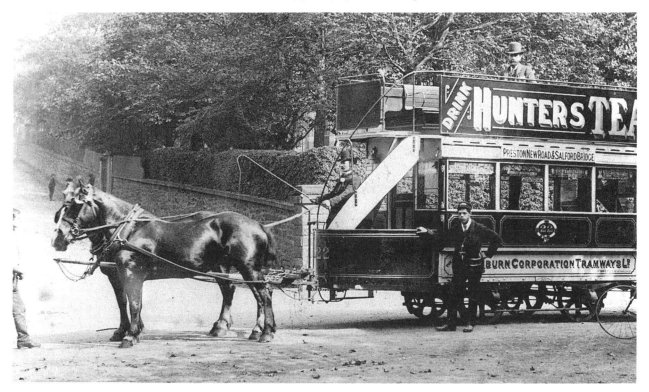

91. Blackburn's tramways were at first operated by a private company which preferred steam trams. The examples have plied the cemetery route.

92. In 1898, Blackburn's tramways were taken over by the Corporation. Electrification was introduced. This 1922 photograph shows the Preston New Road route looking towards Sudell Cross, with a distant tram. Double tracks can be seen in the centre of the road as well as roadside posts to take the overhead lines. Trams remained in use in the town until 1949.

93. As the 1890s Ordnance Survey map of the town centre (illustration 63) reveals, a second market house, bordering Lord Street, was established. An open market area was also laid out and can be seen here as it appeared around 1912.

94 & 95. Two contemporaneous views along King William Street show that the fish market had been rebuilt and that space had been found for additional open stalls.

Market House, and Town Hall   Blackburn.

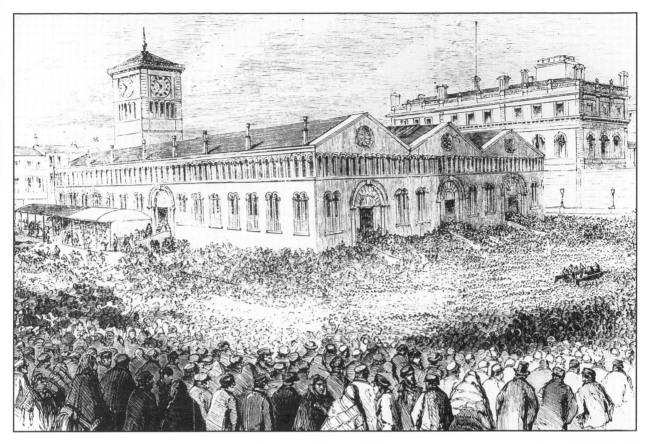

96. Such a large, open space in the town centre could be used for a range of activities, including this meeting of striking operatives. It took place in March 1861.

97. This and the next three photographs give some idea of the type and appearance of shops that developed in Victorian Blackburn as the commercial centre expanded. Church Street, seen here around 1870, had shops which were probably converted from substantial dwelling houses.

98. Victoria Street, shown in this photograph taken around 1906, had impressive three-storeyed shops displaying varied, and at times extravagant, architectural detail.

99. This photograph of Church Street, dating from 1900, again shows stylish commercial premises. They include Thwaites' shopping arcade, with its prominent central gable.

100. This photograph shows the Lord Street frontage of Thwaites' Arcade, looking through to Church Street. Erected in 1883, and named after the prominent local brewing family, the arcade provided undercover shopping in a grand architectural setting. Along with the Victoria Street shops, it fell victim to redevelopment in the early 1970s.

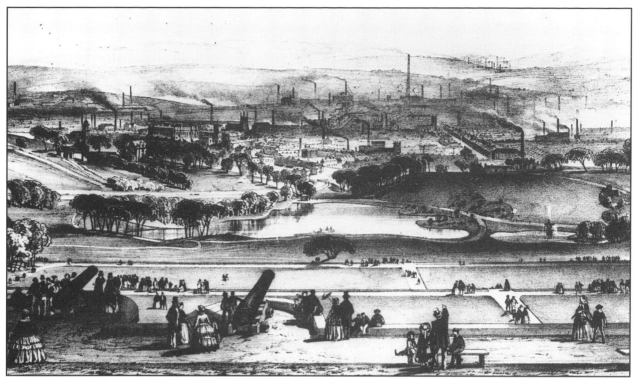

101. Corporation Park, situated on a sloping, 50-acre site above Preston New Road, was opened in 1857. This remarkable illustration, made to commemorate the event, shows the newly laid out Park, with its broad terraces descending the hillside, the uppermost with grid-iron pathways, and those below winding around the slopes and the lakes. Beyond is the central area of the town, with the main buildings clearly shown, and the industrial zone, stretching out along the canal and the valley bottom.

102. This early 20th-century photograph shows the conservatory, one of Corporation Park's most popular attractions.

103. Another was this ornamental fountain, again photographed in the early 1900s. It was one of four presented to the town by the then mayor, William Pilkington.

104. Perhaps the most unusual attraction at Corporation Park was the batteries of cannon, trophies of the Crimean War.

105. Another early 20th-century photograph shows Sunday afternoon crowds along the lower end of Preston New Road, not far from the main entrance to Corporation Park.

106. On special occasions, numbers visiting Corporation Park could be particularly large, as for the dedication of the war memorial, situated in the Garden of Remembrance, in August 1924.

107 & 108. Smaller than Corporation Park and on the opposite side of town, Queen's Park was designated in 1887. One of its main attractions was the boating lake, these early 20th-century photographs recording men at the oars, with women and children being rowed or spectating.

109 & 110. These photographs are of Queen's Park in the early 20th century, showing the boat house and the bowling green.

111. Perhaps Blackburn's most flamboyant building, the Palace Theatre was situated in the Boulevard and was opened as a music hall in 1899. Classical in style and displaying an amazing range of architectural detail, it was criticised by Professor Pevsner because of its 'irresponsible curligigs'. It was demolished in 1989.

112. Another building to be used as a music hall was the Theatre Royal and Opera House in Ainsworth Street. Erected in 1816, it catered at first for middle-class audiences, but turned to more popular entertainment as working-class patronage increased from the 1830s. For details see D. Beattie, *Blackburn; the Evolution of a Lancashire Cotton Town* (1992), p.115. Built in a restrained, classical style, its curved, ashlar frontage added greatly to its visual appeal.

113. The Blackburn Rovers football team in 1882. Both the physical appearance of the players and the informal way they are grouped, suggest a degree of casualness which would not have been inconsistent with the idea that taking part was then more important than winning.

114. The Rovers team in 1889-90, a year they won the F.A. cup. Here they are more formally posed, than in the previous picture, creating a much more purposeful impression. Several players are shown with shin pads worn outside their stockings.

115. This Haworth drawing shows the inlet at Fishmoor reservoir.

116 & 117. The above photograph is of the inlet at Guide reservoir, whilst the photograph below, taken in the 1880s, shows the outlet at Whitendale reservoir.

118. One example of the excreta tub system is shown in this 1879 photograph taken at Waterloo Road, Ewood. Full tubs were extracted through the ground-floor openings in the yard walls, whilst openings at higher level allowed coal to be unloaded into coal houses. The main drawback of the passage was that it was too narrow to take a horse and cart for scavenging purposes.

119. It is plain from this photograph, also taken in 1879, that shared privies could still be found. The privy on the left served four houses, the rear doors of which opened onto the cramped yard. The ground-floor opening at the rear of the privy suggests excreta tubs were in use.

120 & 121. These early 20th-century photographs give some idea of the attractive settings in which the middle-class dwellings were situated. The first is of large, detached dwellings in East Park Road, fronting onto Corporation Park. The second, taken at the junction of Billinge Avenue and Gorse Road, shows houses set in mature, leafy gardens, stretching out along spacious, curvilinear streets.

122 & 123. The earliest middle-class houses in this area, dating from the mid-Victorian years, were mainly built close to the town. Thus, in the first photograph, those on the left were situated just beyond the shops on Preston New Road. As these sites were taken up, more distant ones had to be developed, including those shown in the second photograph. However, the eventual introduction of trams reduced the inconvenience of living at a distance from the town centre.

124. Built from a light-coloured brick with Flemish-bond coursing, Richmond Terrace, completed in 1838, was home to wealthy business and professional people, who might employ several resident servants. The doorways are recessed and have Ionic columns.

125. The gradient on Preston New Road was eased by taking a circuitous route, skirting the hillside rather than surmounting it. Indeed, it was the gentleness of the gradient on Blackburn's early 19th-century turnpike roads which helps to explain why they were chosen as tram routes. Thus, as this early 20th-century photograph shows, the tram route out of town was along Whalley New Road, rather than along Whalley Old Road, with its far steeper gradients. The building in the centre of the picture was a toll house, sited near enough to town to ensure that users of both the old and new routes paid toll, but far enough out so that town traffic would not be charged.

126. Another Blackburn toll bar was located on Preston New Road, at the junction with the present-day ring road. The projecting frontage of the building gave the toll collector clear views along the road. Above the door was a toll board giving the charges. The right to collect tolls on each turnpike road was let by the trustees at annual auctions, so that the risk of generating sufficient income to cover costs was passed to the successful bidder. The photograph was taken in 1890 on the last day tolls were levied.

127 & 128. These photographs, dating from around 1910, are of improved housing at New Bank Road and Preston Old Road, Feniscowles. In both cases, the houses mostly have small front gardens, with low walls and iron railings, at least four fireplaces, back passages, lofty rooms, and restrained decoration. The deep window recesses also indicate cavity walls, a major innovation that was becoming quite common in new housing at this time.

129 & 130. Perhaps the most distinctive of Blackburn's surviving Victorian churches is St Mark's, Buncer Lane. A product of the 1830s, it was built in the then fashionable Romanesque style, an imitation of Roman architecture. (The style is often referred to in this country as Norman.) Key features are round-arched windows, some in groups of three; a tower, situated above the sanctuary, with a gabled, octagonal top and spire; and scalloped friezes.

131. Another impressive Victorian church, designed by the well-known Lancaster firm of Austin and Paley, is St Silas', on Preston New Road. It is built in a perpendicular style, vertical lines appearing in the window tracery. The tower has pinnacles and an octagonal stair turret. The photograph may date from around the time the tower was built in 1913.

132. Whilst Catholic and Anglican church builders favoured Gothic (pointed) architecture, the Nonconformists, in order to be different, were readier to find inspiration in classical architecture. The example shown is the Methodist chapel at Griffin Park, a stone building of three bays and two storeys. Its architectural details, mainly decorated pilasters and round-arched windows with keystones, were concentrated on the upper storey. The photograph dates from the 1880s.

133. This early engraving of the rebuilt parish church probably dates from around mid-century. It can be seen that a decorated style was chosen, the sides supported by pinnacled buttresses, with three-light, transomed windows between. In the clerestory, there are paired windows with trefoil decoration. The prominent west tower contains a lofty, ogee arch, which is recessed and takes the main doorway and a traceried window above.

134. This photograph of the parish church, probably from the early 20th century, shows the south side.

135. The tracery on the nave windows comprises dagger and curved dagger (mouchette) motifs, popular in the early 14th century.

136. This interior view shows nave and chancel arches supported by cylindrical columns, each of which is surrounded by four semi-cylindrical shafts. The ceiling is vaulted (arched) and where it intersects with the short, side vaults from the clerestorey windows (the intersections are called groins), several roof ribs branch out. Where the ribs meet along the length of the roof, elaborate bosses showing fruit, flowers and foliage are evident. The five-light east window with elaborate tracery was set beyond a series of recessed arches. The church also had side galleries and box pews. Social division was reflected in the provision of about half the number of sittings on a free basis. The photograph dates from the early 20th century.

137. Early work on the extension, shown in the photograph, began in the late 1930s, but was delayed by wartime building controls and, subsequently, by the inevitable rise in building costs.

138. The granting of cathedral status to the church in 1926 brought the addition of a new east end. Transepts were added in a similar style to the existing church, dagger motifs again being evident in the window tracery. The sanctuary was sited at the crossing, enabling the service to be seen from nave and transepts. Above the crossing, an octagonal lantern tower was constructed, with pinnacles and a tall, thin spire.

139. The problem of finding sufficient burial space was not resolved until the town's first public cemetery was opened in 1857. Situated off Whalley New Road, it had three chapels and a registrar's house. Its utility to the town is demonstrated by the fascinating statistic that, by 1951, interments had reached no fewer than 176,000, an average of about 1,800 per year (*Barrett's General and Commercial Directory of Blackburn and District*, 1951, p.10). This photograph, *c.*1900, shows one of the chapels and the gates.

140. This photograph of Cicely Bridge Mill was taken in the mid-1980s. Situated alongside the canal, it added a familiar and stylish feature to the skyline above the town centre.

141. In common with many late spinning mills, Imperial Mill was built with a steel frame. As a result, the weight of the building was taken away from the outer walls, so that large window areas could be provided. This gave excellent lighting conditions. The mill was also built on the fireproof principle, so that arched brick roofs and concrete floors replaced the wooden beams, joists and floorboards. The photograph was taken around 1910.

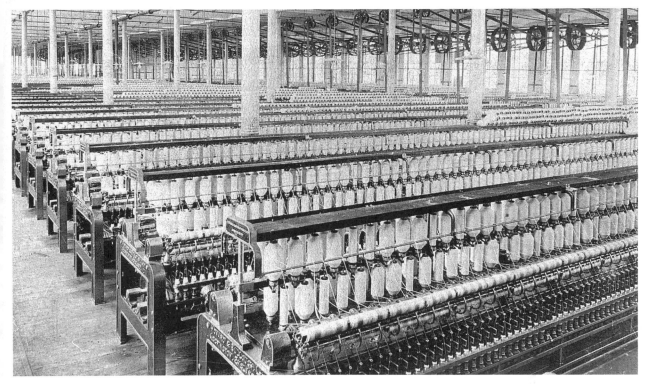

142. The scale of production at the mill is indicated by this photograph showing the vast number of ring spinning spindles on one of the floors. Altogether, there were no fewer than 90,000. For details, see M. Rothwell, *Industrial Heritage: A Guide to the Industrial Archaeology of Blackburn*, part 1 (1985), p.50.

143. Perhaps the most visually-impressive of Blackburn's industrial buildings is Daisyfield Mill, which was used to grind corn. Erected in the early 1870s, it comprises a five-storey block with rows of recessed, round-arched windows. At one end is a massive grain silo, the form and architecture of which resembles that of a Norman castle keep. Use was clearly made of canal facilities, but the mill was also connected to the railway. The photograph was taken around the time that the mill was erected.

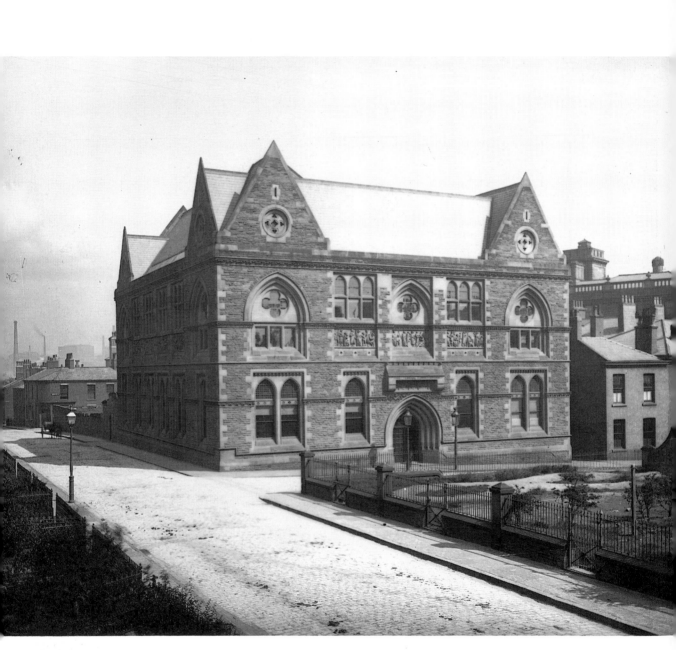

144. The library and museum building was opened in 1874, some 20 years after the town's first free library service had been inaugurated. In Museum Street, the five-bay frontage contains a central doorway with recessed, pointed arches and corbelled canopy above. Grouped lancet windows predominate, several on the first floor having recessed pointed arches with pierced, quatrefoil heads. The photograph was taken around 1880.

145 & 146. Below seven of the first-floor windows are sculptured panels, paid for by leading citizens. Those at the front depict the Arts, Literature and Science, whilst those along the side deal with Industry, Commerce and Agriculture. The photographs show cotton manufacturing and scientific activity.

147 & 148. These carefully-posed photographs show library users in 1926. The reference library was evidently well stocked, though access to some of the volumes and to the long desks would not always have been easy. Children appear to have been important users of library facilities, having their own books, as well as the general stock, on which to draw.

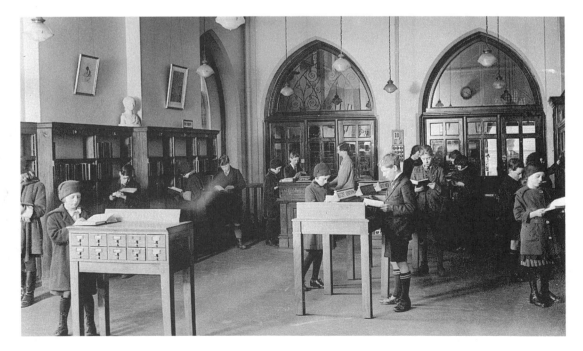

149 & 150. The Cotton Exchange was opened in 1865, its primary function being to provide a weekly meeting place for those engaged in the cotton business. The original design is shown in the above engraving, but, as the early 20th-century photographs on this and the next page reveal, only a shortened octagonal tower and one wing were actually built.

151. The frontage of the wing has five prominent bay-windows, with mullions, transoms and tracery.

152. This painting was executed to commemorate the laying of the foundation stone at the Cotton Exchange in 1863. It was commissioned by the town's leading citizens, who, not surprisingly, stand well to the fore.

153. Completed in 1856, the Town Hall is a three-storey, classical-style building. The frontage has round-arched windows to the lower storeys, those in the end bays being grouped in threes and having a balcony at first-floor level. In the top storey, decorative panels replace windows. There is a prominent cornice above the first-floor windows, with dentil (tooth-like) decoration beneath. The building is surmounted by a balustrade. An unimpressed Nikolaus Pevsner dismissed the building as 'big, Italianate and indifferent'.

154. A key function of the Town Hall has been to act as a focus for major civic occasions, such as the visit of Princess Louise in 1905 to unveil the statue of her mother in the Boulevard.

155 & 156. The connection between royalty and the Town Hall is further reflected in these photographs showing the proclamation of George V's accession in 1910 and the visit of King George V and Queen Mary in 1913 to lay the foundation stone of the public halls.

157. Other local occasions celebrated at the Town Hall include the promotion of Blackburn Rovers to the first division of the Football League in the 1957-58 season.

158. This 1846 illustration of the Bolton, Darwen and Blackburn railway station, situated at Nova Scotia, shows a classical-style building, the main two-storey block having tall windows, a cornice and a hipped roof. To either side were single-storey wings and at the front a *porte cochère* (an open-sided porch wide enough to take wheeled vehicles). During the early 1850s, the station was superseded by that at Stony Butts. Owned by the East Lancashire Railway Company, it was much closer to the town centre.

159. Major extensions and alterations were made to the Stony Butts station during the mid-1880s, especially to the platform structures. Along the length of the frontage, an impressive canopy with a glazed, ridged roof was added. At first-floor level, Venetian windows were incorporated, the central ones with pediments and the outer ones with keystone arches. The alterations brought a fitting addition to the range of visually-striking buildings in the Boulevard and still add architectural distinction to a part of town that, many believe, has scarcely benefited from informed or appropriate planning decisions.

Railway Station, Blackbur

160. Erected in the late 1870s, the Old Bank occupies a prominent site at the junction of Church Street and Darwen Street. An immensely solid-looking building, no doubt designed to inspire depositors' confidence, it has groups of arched windows set high above ground level on both frontages. Above is a cornice and balustrade. The remarkable entrance is set diagonally into a recessed corner, terminating in a lofty, outward-sloping arch. Pevsner regards it as one of Blackburn's best buildings. The photograph was taken in the 1890s.

161. Started in 1888 and not completed until the end of 1894, the Technical School is built mainly of red brick and yellow terracotta. Profusely decorated, it has a symmetrical frontage with the end and central bays standing proud and topped by ornate gables. Much of the decoration, including panels depicting art and craft skills, is displayed on a frieze below the top storey. The centrally-placed doorway has a half-round, keystone arch, the porch of which it forms a part being surmounted by a balustrade with pinnacles at either side. The photograph probably dates from around 1900.

NEW POST OFFICE, BLACKBURN.

162. The post office replaced some rather undistinguished property in Darwen Street, adding notably to the street's architectural quality. Built largely from ashlar, but with some brick, its almost symmetrical façade displays two semi-circular pediments. The ground-floor windows have round arches with keystones. The photograph was probably taken soon after the building was erected.

163. The photograph is of the police station and sessions house soon after it was opened in 1912. The central bays are separated by giant Ionic columns and to either side are rusticated bays containing arched doorways, above which are pedimented windows with balconies. Four-bay, four-storeyed wings complete the building.

Sessions House, Blackburn

164. This photograph shows the Blakey Moor frontage of the public halls. The ground-floor storey is of rusticated stone and the upper storey of ashlar. There is a portico with pairs of fluted, Corinthian columns. The end bays have pilasters and windows framed by columns with sculptures above.

165. This view along Northgate shows that the architectural theme of the Blakey Moor frontage is continued. The building adjoins the police station and sessions house, to which a new southern section was added in the same style. This enabled a gateway to be built into the courtyard. An impressive range of classical-style façades was thereby created. Regrettably, its impact has been muted by an elevated walkway built across Northgate to join the public halls to the present-day library.

166. Three public halls were built, namely the lecture hall, the assembly hall and King George's hall, the first two being equipped with spring floors for dancing. King George's hall, the largest of the three, was designed to accommodate 840 people in its gallery and 1,803 in its main body. Intended to provide space for a wide range of public functions, the halls were pressed into service as a hospital during the Second World War.

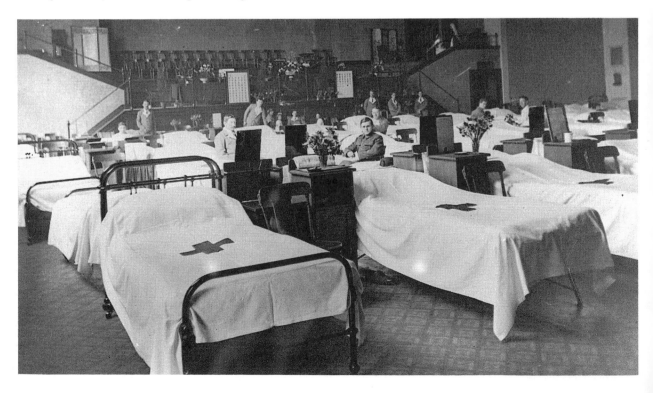

167 & 168. Two major, visually-impressive buildings situated beyond the town centre are the Royal Infirmary and the former workhouse, now Queen's Park Hospital. The Infirmary, financed largely by subscription, was erected during the early 1860s. As this 1910 photograph shows, it consisted of several blocks, placed on either side of a main corridor, so that separate wards were created. Major additions were made to the north end, when the Victoria wing was added in 1897, the Queen's Jubilee year. As the second photograph reveals, these comprise a central, octagonal block, with four-storey wings to either side and a two-storey extension to the front.

169. This photograph shows the large crowds gathered to witness the laying of the foundation stone for the Victoria wing of Queen's Park Hospital.

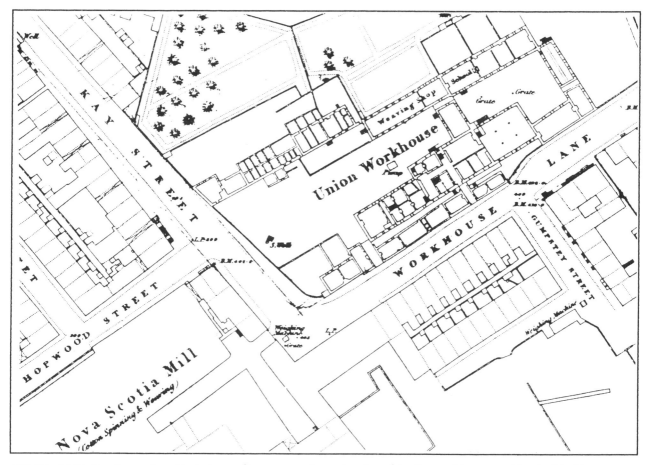

170. The 1840s five feet to the mile Ordnance Survey map shows the plan of the first workhouse used by the Blackburn Poor Law Union. Situated in the Nova Scotia area, it contained a handloom weaving shop as well as a school, suggesting that able-bodied adults and children were amongst the inmates. No doubt, though, both these groups, along with the 'deserving poor' (largely elderly and infirm people), could still obtain out relief. This was especially so during the trade recessions, when too few places would have been available in the workhouse.

171. To provide more adequate levels of accommodation for paupers, a new workhouse was erected on the prominent ridge to the south-east of the town. It comprised an extensive and imposing range of buildings, its physical segregation from the town reflecting that of its inmates from society at large. It could hold no fewer than 700 inmates and cost the then substantial sum of £30,000. Separate facilities were provided for males and females, the fear of reckless breeding amongst paupers appearing as an ever-present threat to the authorities. The photograph probably dates from around 1900.

Conclusion

Throughout much of its history, Blackburn has been a place of no more than local importance, noted largely for its market function and as an ecclesiastical centre. However, its significance rose appreciably during the 17th century when its inhabitants, along with those in the surrounding rural districts, turned increasingly to the manufacture of fustians. By the mid-18th century, the income generated by this industry was having a notable impact on the town's built environment, with a number of large and stylish houses being erected for fustian merchants and manufacturers, principally in King Street. The town had plainly developed a major new function in the production and distribution of textiles, its entrepreneurs operating an extensive putting-out system. That this had taken place well before the classic industrial revolution era, and solely on the basis of hand technology, is all too easily overlooked.

This said, there can be no doubt that Blackburn's emergence as a leading provincial town was closely associated with the rise of the cotton industry. As elsewhere in the Lancashire textile districts, the switch to cotton occurred during the late 18th and early 19th centuries, though factory production remained limited in the town until after the Napoleonic Wars. Indeed, its main physical expansion belonged to the second half of the 19th century, when numerous densely-populated mill communities were created, the western suburbs established and the town centre redeveloped. It was during this period that the town became characterised by grid-iron streets of two-up, two-down houses, surrounding numerous single- and multi-storey cotton mills, the lofty chimneys of which created a particularly striking skyline; it was a townscape that owed far more to functionalism than to visual appeal.

The dominance of cotton in Blackburn's economy did not last, however. During the 20th century, competition from cotton manufacturers in the Far East intensified, forcing an ever-growing number of the town's mills to close. For much of this time, the townscape remained largely unaltered, but during the last 30 years or so, the desire to provide the town with improved facilities and a more up-to-date image has led to redevelopment on a massive scale. As a result, large-swathes of Victorian terraces have been removed; much of the Victorian town centre has been demolished; and the number of cotton mills has shrunk to a handful. To accommodate many of the replacement buildings, whether domestic, industrial or commercial, the town has extended outwards, so that, to a notable degree, its functions have become de-centralised. This has undoubtedly helped to relieve congestion in the town centre. It has also allowed both business owners and customers to indulge their preference for road transport.

How far, on balance, these changes can be seen as beneficial will doubtless continue to be debated. Of course, towns must evolve as circumstances change, so that redevelopment is a necessary, as well as an on-going process. At issue, though, is the pace, scale and type of change. It is here that, in Blackburn's case, there is much cause for concern. If, as has often been observed, Blackburn was not well endowed with many historical buildings of particular merit, then the case for preserving those amongst them that are of the most architectural interest can be seen as being all the stronger. To many, it will seem that such an argument has been used differently, encouraging the view that buildings which are not seen as historically important can be demolished with impunity.

But this line of argument has a further dimension which has been elegantly articulated by one of Blackburn's foremost historians, G. C. Miller. Writing in the *Scapa News Anniversary Number* during the late 1960s, when the town centre was in the throes of redevelopment, he felt entitled to ask whether any of the newly-erected buildings were of outstanding architectural importance. His question was telling, not least because an affirmative response would have given powerful ammunition to those in favour of the redevelopment. Reluctantly, however, he could not give it. He remarked:

> To me it seemed that the new civic centre lacked unity of design. It was little more than a jumble of discordant units whose sole virtues were modernity and utility. There was no wide concept of grandeur or dignity; there was nothing to impress, to uplift, to pass proudly on to posterity. This seemed to me a fatal defect.

A quarter of a century on, his view may still find widespread support.

Blackburn just before the First World War.